Computer by the Tail

Computer by the Tail

A User's Guide to Computer Management

H. DONALDSON
W. G. R. STEVENS
M. I. H. BECKET

He who rides the tiger fears to dismount
Ancient Chinese Proverb

London George Allen & Unwin Ltd
Ruskin House Museum Street

First published in 1976

ISBN 0 04 658220 7

The cartoons by 'Larry' featured in this book are reproduced by kind permission of Leasco Software Limited in whom copyright resides

Printed in Great Britain
in 10 point Times Roman type
by Butler & Tanner Ltd
Frome and London

Contents

Figures

Part I

The Computer Paradox

If you were to ask most *people* for the typical characteristics of computers, the answer would probably be:

'*Speed*: it can perform one million additions per second.'

'*Accuracy*: there are circuits built in to check no mistakes are made. It does not tire like a clerk.'

'*Flexibility*: if the income tax rate is changed it is only necessary to alter one figure in the program.'

'*Large storage facilities*: it is possible to store 25 million characters of information on a single reel of magnetic tape.'

'*Ability to manipulate data at high speed*: invoiced sales can be sorted quickly and analysed by customer, or by representative, or in any other meaningful way.'

'*Ability to evaluate alternative courses of action at high speed*: by simulating years of operation in a few minutes.'

If you were to ask most *managers* what has been their experience of computers, the answer would probably be:

'Invoicing takes longer now than it used to. Under the manual system you could see some results early on, but now we start with nothing, then get everything in one big batch at the end of the day.'

'The statistics are never quite right, either there are items missing or they appear in the wrong place.'

'It takes months to make even the simplest changes to a computer printout.'

'I had much more information on my old stock cards than the computer has now in its stock records.'

'It can't analyse data like a human. For example, it can't seem to see that J. B. Smith of The Larches, 1 High Street, is the same man as John Smith, The Larches, High Street. And it can't spot an obvious trend slightly different from the one we asked about.'

'Some of its solutions are quite unworkable in practice – my people can almost always improve on them.'

This then is the computer paradox: it works at high speed yet is slow to produce results; it is very accurate but the answer is not always right; it is flexible if the problem has been anticipated but desperately inflexible if not; it can store large quantities of information but never enough.

The purpose of this book is to explain the paradox and to give executives a feel for suitable and unsuitable application areas.

This book is for people who are not computer professionals – and do not want to be – but who come into contact with, or find themselves in charge of, computers during their working life. It is more cautious – perhaps gloomy – than most books about computers in business.

Chapter 1

Man and Machine

Over a century ago Charles Babbage invented the 'analytical engine', the mechanical predecessor of the computer – and Lady Lovelace wrote of it at the time:

'It is desirable to guard against the possibility of exaggerated ideas that might arise as to the powers of the analytical engine. In considering any new subject there is frequently a tendency, first, to overrate what we find already interesting or remarkable; and secondly, by a sort of natural reaction, to undervalue the true state of the case when we do discover that our notions have surpassed those that were really tenable. The analytical engine has no pretensions whatever to originate anything. It can do whatever we know how to order it to perform.'

Every word applies to present-day computers. We, too, have gone from enthusiastic wonder to disillusion – both of them exaggerated – and many people are only just beginning to realise that computers will do only what they are told. That is quite a useful attribute but, to managers who expected miraculous instant solutions to all business problems, efficient docility is not enough. The consequent reaction has been that the computer is an expensive confidence trick.

No amount of faith will persuade a computer to work miracles.

When one looks into the much publicised computer failures and the innumerable horror stories, most cases of disaster and of inefficiency turn out to stem from an elementary misunderstanding of what a computer is, what it can do, and what it is good at. In other words, whenever a manager is blaming a computer he is in fact exposing his own ignorance. But strangely enough the man who rants at the problems a computer causes would not think of attacking a complex machine tool because it failed to open a tin of beans, yet often that is the sort of problem confronting him.

Basically a computer is a complicated piece of electronic circuitry with one major advantage: it can quickly carry out many calculations. But it is a stupid machine: it knows nothing except what the user tells it; it cannot show any initiative but must blindly follow instructions; and it cannot spot even obvious mistakes unless someone has patiently explained the logic of what constitutes an obvious mistake (which is harder than it sounds – try it).

From this follows the old computer man's adage – *garbage in, garbage out*. In other words, the information coming out is totally dependent on the information going in, and on what the computer has been told to do with it. And those instructions must be far more comprehensive than the instructions to a clerk, for even the dimmest human starts off with some experience and common sense.

It is already becoming clear that there will be some jobs a computer will do economically and others it would either make a complete mess of, or in which it would just prove a totally unjustifiable expense. For instance, it is obviously not reasonable to put a rapidly changing job or a one-off job on to a computer, for the explanations of how to do it might take longer than the job itself.

Different abilities of men and machines indicate which sort of job each is best at:

Human	*Computer*
Can see overall problems, wider contexts, tacit relationships.	Can cope with complex problems but only where all the parameters have been completely specified.
Can spot obvious nonsense either in input or in output, and can adapt to changing circumstances.	Continues to apply rules until told otherwise and hence cannot see when rules are no longer relevant.
Is flexible in work; can adapt to the unexpected and can fairly easily be reallocated to new jobs.	Can only handle exceptions it has been told to expect; lengthy and expensive to reallocate to new tasks.
Can learn from experience, can use initiative.	Can only apply rules it has been explicitly told.
Performance variable but seldom wholly accurate and hence not completely predictable.	Always consistent.

Large but non-specific and unreliable memory.	Smaller total memory but can be more extensive on specifics and more reliable.
Slow in performing complex routine calculations and in complicated data handling.	Fast in routine tasks no matter how complex.
Unpredictable in cost, efficiency, and up-time (time wasted as percentage of potential working hours).	Predictable cost, reasonably predictable efficiency and up-time.
Subtle but imprecise communication ability.	Limited but precisely defined communication ability.

There is, however, a similarity between clerks and computers. For example, a clerk sitting at a desk to calculate the weekly payroll would start with the attendance record for each man, locate his file history (which gives total gross pay to date and tax paid so far), and obeying a set of rules would calculate the pay due, writing the result on a payslip.

* The attendance records are the input of new information
* The file history is the existing information changed by updating which gets it ready for the following week
* There are rules for the clerk to follow – though some may not be totally spelled out – and the clerk remembers them
* The calculation is one man at a time
* There is an output in the form of a payslip

Compare the computer. It actually does a very similar job to the clerk, using input, storage, calculation and output in a similar manner.

* Input comes through such devices as card readers, paper tape readers, magnetic ink character readers, etc.
* Storage or memory would be in devices such as magnetic discs or tapes
* Calculations are done within the central processing unit which is the equivalent of the clerk's mind
* Output comes from equipment such as line or character printers, or cathode ray tubes (these, like the input devices, are known as peripherals)

A clerk can do a number of different jobs. By changing the instructions to follow, the same clerk can start on a completely new job such as invoicing. In the same way, by changing the computer's job instructions, called the program (now an accepted British spelling for this use), it too can do a different job. A computer will have a library of such programs.

Like the clerk, the computer does each job one at a time, e.g. calculates each man's pay in turn. So the number of men on the payroll will not affect the size of processor needed – since the job is done one man at a time, adding 10 per cent to the number of people to

Computers are not the universal answer to business problems

be paid will merely add 10 per cent to the time taken for processing, not to the size of machine required.

So a computer is a patient, plodding but efficient machine which can supplement human ingenuity but not supplant it. In some ways it can automate the repetitive work that clerks do but is seldom a direct replacement. It follows that the tasks to which it is applied must be very carefully scrutinised and the process of transference strictly controlled – in other words, for efficient use, both the machine and its specialists need rigorous management control.

Bear in mind the following points:

1. Most computer systems do not live up to expectations – perhaps the expectations were unrealistically high, but that is part of the point.
2. Many computers – estimates range from 40 per cent to 60 per cent – are not economically sound investments in the sense of making a net contribution to the owner's profits (some have in fact lost their owners millions of pounds).
3. Computers are not the universal answer to business problems. They have advantages and disadvantages which vary from application to application, but for the moment the more extravagant claims, like 'computers are to business what the nervous system is to the body', remain in the realm of science fiction.

Note: Although the book concentrates on business and most of the examples are drawn from there, the same criteria, the same controls and the same disciplines are applicable to other computer users from government departments to universities.

Chapter 2

What is a Suitable Computer Application?

There are two parts to making a job successful on the computer: the first is to pick a suitable application, the second is to ensure it works properly on the computer. The first will be dealt with in this chapter, the second in Chapter 5.

The moral of the previous chapter is that computers are highly efficient at some tasks and hopelessly time-wasting and uneconomical at others.

Many suitable applications have turned out to be disastrous through incompetent implementation, and many highly unsuitable applications are well thought of because they are working without giving trouble (though this often stems from a lack of management criteria for success).

Subjective opinions on what is a suitable application are, despite their common usage, unlikely to be a reliable guide. Nor can one catalogue the most suitable areas (though again many do) since what is right for one company may be completely wrong for another. Every organisation is different and hence it has different needs – different efficiencies or different management attitudes can affect suitability. So all we can do is to provide guidelines on the symptoms of jobs which might work, and of those to avoid completely.

One guide for an organisation trying computers for the first time is to start with applications which are apparently simple and have a readily attainable tangible payoff. It is important that even the first appliction pays, for the computer department quickly gets into disrepute if it is not seen to be doing a good commercial job. The first application often sets the pattern for the remainder, and there is little evidence to suggest that a series of loss-making applications can add up to a profitable whole.

There are easy ways to spot possible areas for computerisation: where large numbers of clerical staff are employed, where the present system is hard to run, where space is limited, where there is a shortage of the right sort of staff or they have become very expensive, where there is a need to expand the business, and so on. But having found applications which seem to have computer potential, one must rank them by priority (by intensity of problem, minimum risk of failure, or major savings attainable), and then examine each of them to gauge whether it is in fact suitable.

So one company may start with sales statistics since there are clear gains and invoicing is complex, and another with order processing since this provides the information for stock control where the major financial benefits are seen to lie. Other potential application areas are invoicing, sales ledger, stock recording, stock control, bill of materials, production planning, cash flows and wages calculations.

Do not be fooled, though, by claims that some areas are natural computer projects. Every organisation must check its own procedures and costs, to find the benefits. What is a roaring success in one company can be a disastrous failure in another, because, even if the general area looked suitable, the circumstances can prevent efficient transfer of the problem to computers.

There are seven key factors which govern the profitable use of computers:

1. Ratio of input to output
2. Degree of organisational integration achieved
3. Amount of file maintenance
4. Difficulty of pinning down the rules
5. The degree of involvement of user managers
6. State of the present system
7. Value for money

To find if a particular computer application you have in mind is suitable in practice, check it against each of these criteria on the following pages and score it as indicated. Use Figure 2 to record your scores and compare the final result with the rating scale on page 35.

When you have got the rating, discuss it with the office manager and/or the computer staff – they have different and possibly simpler ways of approaching the problem. Incidentally, the same principles apply whether it is for using an in-house computer or linking into a bureau, though the costs of hardware would be different.

This is obviously not the whole story and a decision to go ahead or not can patently not be taken on the evidence of these scores alone. But the analysis will show whether the application you have in mind has the odds on its side, and will also show where the main dangers can lie if a go-ahead is authorised.

RATING YOUR APPLICATION AREAS

1. RATIO OF OUTPUT TO INPUT

Overall, input is probably the highest cost area in business data processing, a problem we explore further in Chapter 6. Transcribing everyday documents like customer orders, employee attendance records and stock movement slips into a form suitable for computers to read is both costly and duplicates effort.

The first measure, therefore, of suitability is to judge how often the input is to be used once it is in the system. Here are some guidelines:

Sales statistics

Sales statistics tend to be suitable for computers because the same basic information is often needed in many different sequences. The computer can produce sales analyses:

* by product group within representative
* by product group within customer class
* by customer class within representative

Each of these uses the basic invoiced sales information in a different way. Note that a summary report does not count as an additional output to a more detailed report.

In measuring the ratio of output to input, consider only that output you *know* you want rather than what you *think* you might want. One way to think about that distinction is to check how often you have recently found the information indispensable.

Consider only the expensive 'prime' input; input which has to be punched into cards or tape, keyed on to magnetic tape or disc, or read optically. Do not consider input from 'turnaround' punched cards, by-product paper tape from an accounting machine, nor input from another computer procedure.

The general rule is that 'prime' input is so expensive that if the information is not used at least three times, it is not worth putting into the computer.

By these criteria, 'sales statistics' qualifies as a worthwhile 'stand alone' application. The input is used at least three times. It is even more worthwhile if the sales information comes from the invoicing procedure on the computer. In this case the input comes for no additional cost.

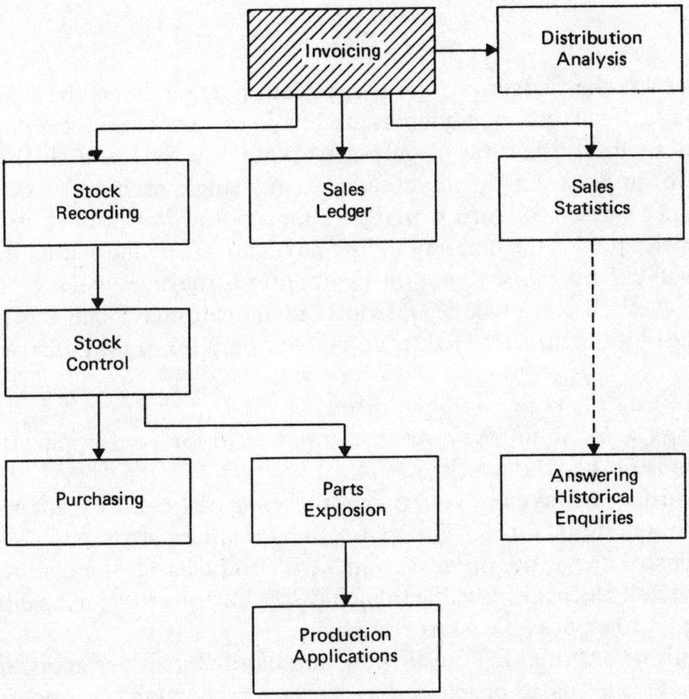

FIG. 1 Invoicing: The Starting Point for Many Applications

Invoicing

On the other hand, invoicing can hardly ever be justified as a 'stand alone' procedure. The ratio of output to input is not much better than 1 to 1. You must feed in customer code for the computer to print the name and address. For every item ordered you must feed in the product code and quantity for the computer to print the line and extend the value.

The reason invoicing (or order processing) is often done on the computer is because it is the application which triggers so many other applications:

Stock recording and stock control
Sales statistics
Sales ledger
Distribution analysis
Answering historical enquiries

Sales ledger
Whether sales ledger is a good application depends on the system you use. If customers' payments are linked to specific invoices ('open item' method) the ratio of output to input is 1 to 1 and so this is a poor application. At the other extreme, single cash entry with a balance carried forward would give high output to input ratio but the price paid is the inability to link payment to any individual item. A useful compromise to put on a computer is the 'aged balance' system which carries a balance forward but allocates payments received to the oldest item on the ledger unless the computer is told otherwise.

Improving the output to input ratio
Having worked out the output to input ratio for your application, there is no need to accept it.

If orders are taken by your own representatives, can they not mark computer input forms? Computer mark readers are relatively inexpensive and if the order document is produced on the computer in the first place it is possible to include the customer code and eliminate another possible source of error.

This sort of thinking must be the aim of all system designers. Can input be eliminated or reduced to exception reporting? Is it possible to use computer output again as input? Can the cycle between document origination and computer input be reduced?

We can now begin to develop a scale for judging the overall suitability of an application to a computer. The first stage in this assessment is to use the chart in Figure 2 against 'Ratio of Output to Input' to score:

0 if the output/input ratio is 1 to 1 or less (e.g. open-item sales ledger)

4 if the output/input ratio is 2 to 1 (e.g. aged balance sales ledger)

6 if the ratio is 3 to 1 (e.g. 'stand-alone' sales statistics)

10 if the ratio is 5 to 1 or better (e.g. sales statistics as a by-product of invoicing)

KEY FACTOR	Application Area														
1. Ratio of Output to Input															
2. Degree of Integration															
3. Amount of File Maintenance															
4. Complexity of Problem Definition															
5. Likely Involvement of User Manager															
6. State of Present System															
7. Value for Money															
TOTAL															

FIG. 2: How Suitable is Your Proposed Computer Application?
Use this form to assess whether your application area is suited to computer processing. Application areas include order processing, invoicing, sales ledger, sales statistics, stock recording, stock control, parts explosion, production planning, renewals, deposit accounts, etc. A guide to the method of scoring is in the text.

2. DEGREE OF INTEGRATION ACHIEVED

Figure 1 showed that invoicing can be the starting point for a great number of different applications. Although it can rarely be judged a suitable application on its own it can sometimes be justified by the degree of integration it achieves – the inter-linking of the company's different administrative problems. This integration of an organisation's activities obviously produces its own efficiencies.

Another example is labour/job costing. It is the basic application from which calculating gross pay by hours worked at various rates, job costing and operating statements can be prepared.

However, neither application has to be done on a computer (Figure 3 shows how computer input can be captured either before, during, or after invoicing). Nevertheless, there are advantages in using the computer. For the same input effort you can carry out an additional application. The second stage of assessing the suitability of the application is to score:

0 if no integration is achieved

5 if integration is achieved

3. AMOUNT OF FILE MAINTENANCE

Almost all computer applications involve setting up 'files'. For example, lists of customer names and addresses for invoicing and sales ledger; product descriptions and prices for invoicing and stock recording; employee records for payroll. Whenever there is a file, programs must be written to keep the file up to date and to correct errors.

Some files are relatively static – like name and address files. Some are modified fairly frequently – like the records of monthly-paid staff who have tax code changes, alterations to deductions, and salary reviews. Some records are constantly modified – like the details of casual labour on a building site.

So the next stage in assessing the application is to make an estimate of the average number of records modified whenever the file is used.

Score:

–10 if the ratio is 1 for 1 e.g. payroll for casual labour

0 if the ratio is 1 in 2 records modified each cycle

2 if the ratio is 1 in 4 records modified e.g. monthly payroll

4 if the ratio is 1 in 6 records modified or fewer e.g. names and addresses

4. DIFFICULTY OF PINNING DOWN THE RULES

One of the major problems of using computers profitably lies in 'pinning down the rules', especially when wide discretion is allowed to

BEFORE INVOICING

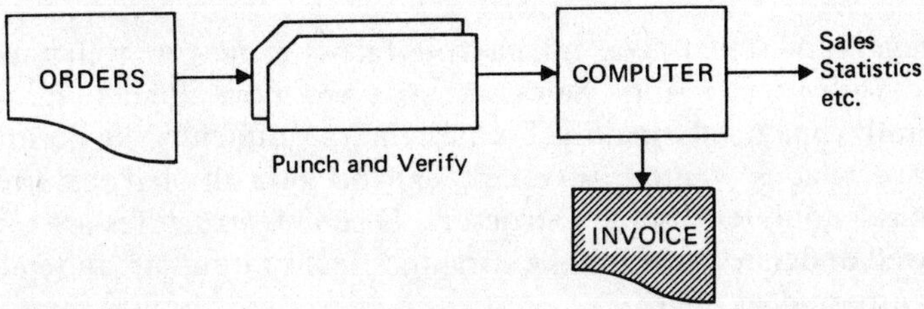

Orders can be coded, punched and verified and the cards then used as computer input. The computer can then generate Invoices, Sales Statistics etc. For standard products, coding, punching and verifying can be replaced by 'pulling' pre-punched master cards.

DURING INVOICING

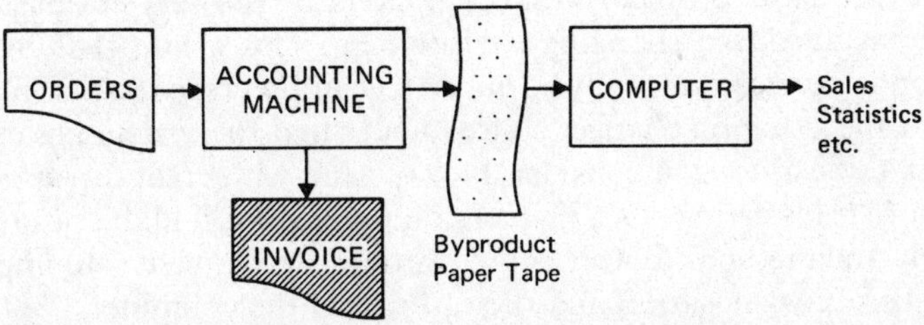

Invoices can be prepared on an accounting machine or electric typewriter and a byproduct paper tape created at the same time. This paper tape can be used as computer input (your own computer or a service bureau) for the computer to generate Sales Statistics etc.

AFTER INVOICING

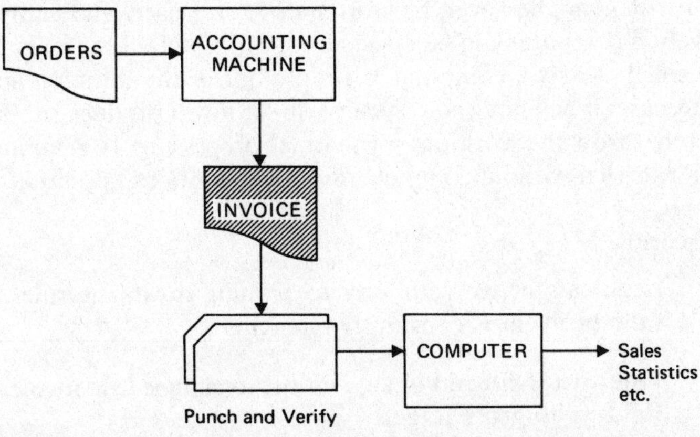

Invoicing can be carried out using address plates or a simple typewriter. Cards are punched from the Invoice and are used to generate Sales Statistics etc.
In general Invoicing can be a good computer application if there is a high volume and standard product lines. Low volume or non-standard product lines make a poor application.

FIG. 3 Capturing Computer Input

managers and staff. In general, payrolls (gross-to-net) are well understood with precise rules. Sales statistics are more difficult than is generally imagined – mainly because of the difficulty in deciding exactly what is wanted. Invoicing can be difficult – particularly if there is a complex discount structure. Discount structures are often not well understood within the firm and tend to build up anomalies over a period of time.

Although invoicing will always tend to be a more difficult area than payroll, the problem can usually be improved. Before deciding on a computer, the discount structure should be streamlined to reduce anomalies.

Another major problem is that computers are not very flexible and so are unsuited to a changing environment. This means that either the application cannot really be put on to computers in the first place or that the situation changes so frequently that the system has constantly to be altered at considerable cost and with great disruption.

Before transferring work on to a computer it must all be rational, orderly and methodical. Occasionally, the wisest course is to implement this reorganisation and then to cancel the computer.

There is a good deal of truth in our adage that 'no progressive company can afford to have a computer'. So look ahead and estimate the future needs both for growth and for flexibility; if change is likely to be considerable you might well find people adapt with less difficulty than electronic machines.

If the rules can, however, be written down precisely and comprehensively, a computer can be considered. But if not all the rules can be specified clearly a computer is simply out of the question since in many cases it will not know what to do, or it will produce rubbish, or merely throw the work out for manual processing. It is a fundamental rule that without complete rules computers can do no useful work.

So score:

– 100 if you cannot see your way to pinning down the rules, or if the problem is constantly changing

0 if the area is difficult or susceptible to change (e.g. invoicing, build-up-to-gross wage)

5 if the area is well understood but no standard manuals exist describing the present system

10 if the area is well understood and standard manuals exist (e.g. payroll gross-to-net)

5. LIKELY INVOLVEMENT OF USER MANAGERS

The success of a computer application depends to a large extent on the involvement of the managers whose staff will use the system.

In one manufacturing company there was constant friction between the computer department and the line functions of the company. There were faults on both sides, but responsibility was finally pinned down to the line functions.

The problems they wanted the computer people to solve were often not thought through, but more importantly the computer department lacked the specialist knowledge of the function.

The difficulty was solved in this company by supplying project leaders from the appropriate function to be responsible for the problem definition through to implementation.

The success of a computer application depends to a large extent on the involvement of the managers whose staff will use the system

In assessing your application, assess what involvement you can expect from your line managers in both helping to specify the application and seeing it through to implementation.

Score:

– 10 if the computer department is to be left on its own to get on with it

0 if the manager with the required knowledge is very busy

10 if an able member of the user department is to take responsibility for applying the computer within his function

6. STATE OF THE PRESENT SYSTEM

O & M and computer analysts are often called in to help where there are problems. When the dust has settled after they have introduced improvements, what do we see? All too often the areas which were *not* giving problems have been improved (they are easier to improve) but the real problems tend to remain.

It is also unfortunately true that computer systems are most successful in organisations which are already efficient. This is because computers require a tightly disciplined approach with exceptions kept to a minimum and accurate recording of information.

If the operation of existing systems is slack, introducing a computer will not help. It usually makes matters far worse.

For example, a storekeeper can usually tell from the description if the wrong code is attached. But if a computer is given the wrong code it will generate the wrong description as well. It thus makes it almost impossible to pick up this type of error before the customer is sent the wrong goods.

So score:

0 if the existing clerical procedures are inefficient or error prone

5 if they are fairly good

10 if they are as good as O & M and logic can make them

The lesson here is that it is unsound to go from a poor manual system directly to a computer. This short cut is hardly ever successful. It is prudent (and often indispensable) to clean up the existing procedures first and then consider the computer.

7. VALUE FOR MONEY

Investing in computers is a costly business so here are some final points to discover whether the value obtained is worth the money invested.

The first point to check is whether you can see a return on your investment. If you have managed to get all the other points looking good, the chances are you will be getting value for money. After all, what makes computers economically worthwhile is the ability to do quickly the work many clerks would take a long time to produce, and the ability to allow managers to control an organisation more precisely. If you can achieve this, and the task is the sort that in your particular outfit can be put on to a computer easily, the auguries are good.

But it is still worth a double check. Calculate the cost of the present system both in direct terms such as wages, stationery and overheads, and in indirect terms such as training new staff, stoppages, loss of customers through slowness or inefficiency, etc. Then do a comparable analysis of the computer costs: rental charges, or the opportunity costs of the capital for purchase plus depreciation, overheads, stationery, staff costs.

Most companies selecting computers do so on the basis of the cost of the computer itself – the hardware; but some studies in the United States show that for every $100 spent on computers (for equipment, buildings, maintenance), the user must spend another $200 running them (for systems analysts, programmers and operators). Our experience suggests a typical cost breakdown along the lines in Figure 4.

So calculate the real costs and quantified benefits which will result from the change.

Tangible benefits

Most cost justifications for computer systems contain some of the following items, but to be worth considering they must have cash values attached to them.

The cost ratios below are based on a medium-sized computer which will be run for two shifts five days per week. Included in the staff are six punch and verifier operators. The computer is on a five-year rental agreement and other capital items are depreciated over five years.

Operating Costs (running the computer)	
Computer	1000
Ancillary equipment	150
Employment costs (19 staff)	900
Running costs	700
Accommodation and installation	400
	3150
Systems Analysts, Programmers, O & M	
Employment costs (21 staff)	1400
Accommodation and office equipment	900
	2300
Cost of whole department	5450

So for every £1000 of computer you can expect to spend another £2300 on staff, £1300 on accommodation and £850 on running costs. The computer is less than 20 per cent of the total.

FIG. 4 Typical Computer Cost Ratios

1. Reduced clerical staff costs as a proportion of total costs. These are notoriously difficult to achieve in practice, as jobs tend to be found for displaced staff. They can most often be achieved when a company is expanding; it is easier to control the take-on of new staff than to reduce staff numbers.

2. Better inventory control with less capital tied up in stock. This is achieved very frequently although it tends to be due to the introduction of a sound system rather than with a computer, and often costs more than it should.

3. Better sales ledger control with less capital tied up in debts. Again, frequently achieved, but sometimes at too great a cost.

4. Improved customer service by reducing the lead time on orders. One note of caution: it sometimes happens that the lead time of the majority of orders is reduced only at the expense of increasing the lead time on urgent orders.

Intangible benefits

Tangible benefits shade off into the so-called 'intangible benefits', which are real but which cannot have a cash value assigned to them. For example, it can be argued that improved customer service, listed above as 'tangible', is really intangible, as it is very much a matter of opinion to what extent it will increase sales and hence profits.

Claims about improved customer service should be treated with scepticism unless backed by specific instances of orders lost, improvements unrealised, debts uncollected, or whatever. And even if instances are found it is worth checking whether a computerised system would have avoided them.

A common justification for using a computer is better information for management. Often this does actually come about, but (see Chapter 3) equally often it does not. Certainly, it is always worthwhile to seek the opinion of the managers who will be using the information in question, before taking a decision on this issue.

If it is claimed for instance that managers or supervisors will have more time for other things, one must ask what things. In other words what work is currently being neglected, and how much is that neglect costing the company. (This may produce valuable spinoffs in testing whether managers' priorities are right.)

If staff morale or satisfaction is the claim, ask what changes in staff turnover might be expected and what the financial benefits of that would be.

If the residuals remain stubbornly intangible they are unlikely to be benefits. Money is tangible.

Even if the company is only renting a computer and not buying one, considerable costs have to be incurred before there is any return. A typical, though simplified, cash flow pattern in a case where a medium-sized computer was successfully installed is shown in Figure 5. Referring to the numbers in the diagram:

1. The decision is taken to investigate the possible use of a computer.

2. The decision is taken to go ahead – note how little expenditure has been incurred at that time. The order is placed for the equipment.

3. Extra staff are recruited and the design and programming of the first system proceeds.

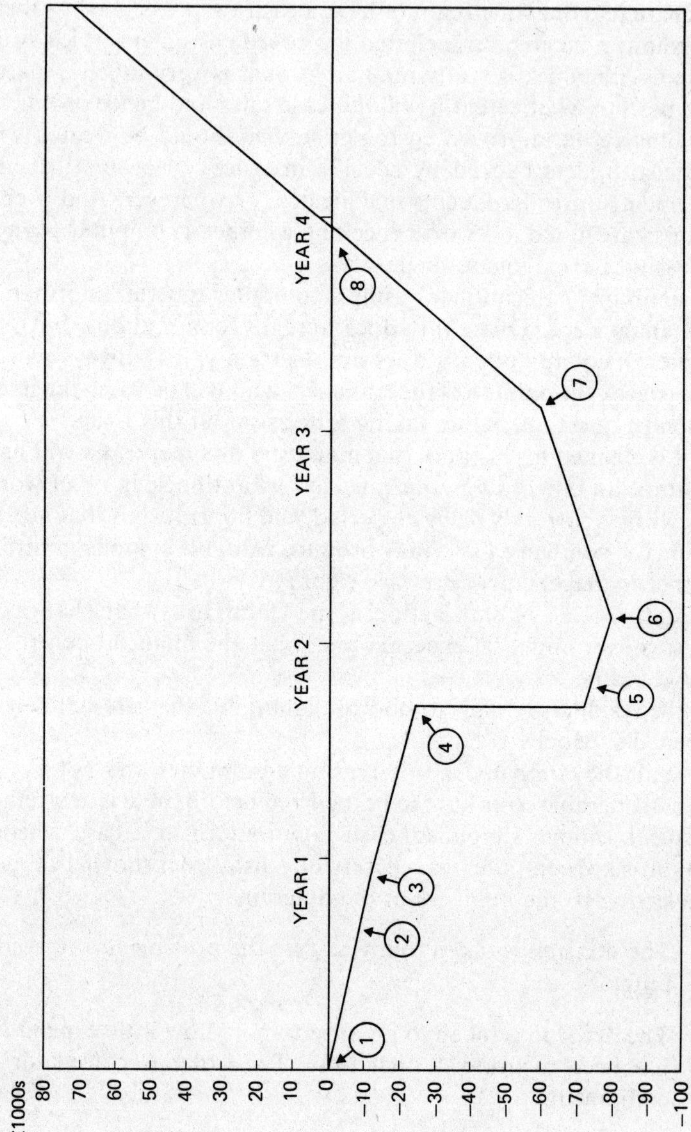

FIG. 5 Cumulative Costs of a Computer Project

4. The equipment is installed and paid for.

5. The first system is completed and –

6. becomes operational.

7. The second system becomes operational.

8. After four years the breakeven point is reached.

This is a highly satisfactory result in view of the fact that the computer, with several years of useful life left, is producing nett benefits at a rate of £70,000 per year. However, it should be noted that over two years passed and a total of £80,000 was spent before any benefits at all were achieved. Also, no allowance has been made for the interest on the capital needed nor the opportunity costs.

Tangible costs

The tangible costs of a computer installation will include all or some of the following:

1. Main-frame computer costs. Computers and most of the associated equipment can be purchased outright, taken on a long or medium-term lease, or rented.

2. Peripheral equipment costs. A computer will have a number of peripherals (readers, printers, etc.) and also, perhaps, remote terminals.

3. Data preparation equipment, i.e. card or tape punches and verifiers.

4. Site preparation, probably including air conditioning, and then space costs.

5. Staff costs, i.e. managers, analysts, programmers, computer operators, punch operators.

6. Software costs, some of which may be included within the basic computer cost.

7. Maintenance of all equipment.

Intangible costs

When people attempt to evaluate whether a computer should be used, they will always include tangible costs and tangible benefits in the analysis, and, almost always, intangible benefits. Intangible costs are almost never included. These include:

1. Loss of flexibility. Computer systems are always less flexible than clerical systems, and this serious drawback can turn out to be very costly.

2. Loss of skilled staff. Computer projects always demand the attention and time of able and experienced personnel at all levels in the organisation. Since these able people generally have their hands full already, a computer project will cause some other activity to suffer.

Having established the tangible and intangible costs and benefits it is time to try your own cash flow calculations, including not just the hardware but programming, organisation and management costs as well. Be very wary of projects which produce no measurable improvements (return on capital invested) for a long time. Benefits are elusive at the best of times and become rapidly more so as the results get more distant. So try to get some benefits or return within about twelve months.

Compare the costs of buying, renting and using a bureau. Will you be getting a return in a year?

It is important to know how long you could expect to keep the present system and hence how long the computer might be used. Check that the flexibility needed is not greater than the computer can cope with, and also see how long you need to write off the machine and its software. In other words: is the present or planned system able to cope with the foreseeable changes?

Are you sure computers are the cheapest way of solving the problem? Rather than install a costly and sophisticated computer to handle debtors it might be wiser to hire a first-rate credit controller. In other words, check the cost/benefit calculations of alternative solutions – computer experts often recommend a complex solution but a prudent manager should opt for most of the benefits (if not all) at a lower risk.

Incidentally, computers are often promoted on the basis of their speed. But this normally refers only to the central processing unit whereas the speed of the whole installation is limited more by the speed of the peripherals, or even more importantly by the speed of the data preparation girls, the output clerks distributing the results, and the speed of the control clerks and coders. These people affect the speed of the complete system and it is on the basis of them and the work they have to do that the speed of the installation must be calculated.

All of which brings us back to the fundamental question: are you certain computers are the real answer to your real problems? Are you sure you could not manage without a computer?

Here are the four questions again:

(*a*) Can you see a return on your investment?

(*b*) Will you be getting some benefit or return within twelve months?

(*c*) Is the planned system able to cope with foreseeable changes?

(*d*) Have you realistically considered alternatives to the computer?

For every 'no' to these questions, subtract 5 from your score.

HOW DID YOU SCORE?

The total number of points from each heading gives an indication of the suitability for an application to go on to the computer. So now compare each application score with the rating.

Any area that scored less than 25 starts off with the odds heavily against it. It is a poor application area and best avoided.

Between 30 and 40 the application is worth thinking about, it sounds a reasonable proposition.

Anything over 40 seems almost too good to be true. Nothing is that perfect – are you sure you have answered the questions honestly? If, after rational reconsideration, the score is still high, you seem to be on to a winner.

But these scores are based on existing procedures or at best a tidied version of them, so do not accept a low score. Think again. As the chapter has shown, there is an awful lot you can do to improve the scores and hence the chances of using a computer profitably – or even of profitably doing without a computer by organising sensibly.

Here are the main points again:

1. Reduce input to a minimum by using exception reports, turn-around documents, and by-product input.

2. Pin down the processing rules precisely *before* embarking on using a computer – not after.

3. Ensure line managers retain responsibility for the successful introduction of computer systems.

4. Make sure the existing systems are sound and error-free before converting to a computer.

5. Make sure you are getting value for money – in the short term.

Which all explains the point of the saying – 'Don't just computerise your existing manual procedures'. In most companies there is a lot of work to be done before they are ready for computers. But this is not work without rewards. You should set a target of improving every area by 20 per cent. Aim for either a 20 per cent cost reduction in the present system or a 20 per cent increase in throughput at the same cost.

Do not imagine that this sort of appraisal technique is necessary only when deciding on the initial acquisition of a computer. It applies equally to every subsequent job to be put on it, and to enhancements and replacements. Once the computer is there, both computer people and departmental managers will start suggesting some pieces of work be shunted on to the electronic miracle clerk.

If you do decide to get your own computer, judge the size very carefully. You should have outline plans for at least the next stage in the computerisation process, and so will have some idea whether more work is due to go on to the machine and when. From there it is possible to deduce how much slack the current model should have to accommodate the extra work.

This sort of thing can also be costed out, and should be. If the computer is working at only 60 per cent of capacity, then 40 per cent of the investment is wasted. If it takes, say, three years before the excess capacity begins to be utilised, one can calculate the real cost of that 40 per cent tied-up capital over three years, then compare it with the costs of buying a smaller computer and transferring later to a larger model. Both should be compared with the costs incurred by delaying computerisation of the work and of starting with a bureau.

Some companies decide to go for the biggest, newest machine on the principle that one can always find work for the spare capacity

While it can be disruptive to buy a small inflexible system and incur the possible complications of later enhancements or replacements, buying a machine that is much too big can be equally difficult.

Some companies decide to go for the biggest, newest machine on the principle that one can always find work for the spare capacity. This can lead to an unprofitable investment at best and enormous problems at worst. The computer is often wastefully used and new additional projects fail to get this Chapter 2-type rigorous screening for usefulness and financial viability. The results can even be counter-productive, being more difficult to control.

Another course large-pursed buyers sometimes follow is to sell spare computer time on a bureau basis. Such ventures seldom prosper.

The bureau work is usually not properly costed and is therefore charged on a marginal cost basis. That will lessen the justification for the original computer purchase. Another point is that this is a diversification into a highly specialised service industry, of which companies normally working in other fields are ignorant. Diversification strategy needs very careful consideration and usually should capitalise on existing talents and experience. Going into computer bureaux is unlikely to do this.

Incidentally, another prospect companies could bear in mind is that it is not always necessary to buy new computers – some recent ranges are still perfectly usable but very much cheaper.

To give you a flavour of the way these factors can come together in real life, here are a couple of examples which are drawn from actual companies, though they have been disguised for the illustration. As an exercise consider the facts and see what you would do and then check to see if your conclusions match our analysis.

CASE STUDY 1 – DELIA PLANT HIRE (DPH)

BACKGROUND

DPH, part of the Delia Group, hires out plant and vehicles on contract. About 60 per cent of these contracts are for twelve months or longer, while most of the remaining business is 'spot hire'. The basis of the contract is a monthly standing charge plus a rate based on usage (miles run or hours switched on). Usually a driver or operator is supplied with the plant.

DPH has a combined head office and depot with four additional depots throughout the country. These depots are used to store plant and vehicles not in use and also to carry out routine maintenance. Major repairs are carried out at the head office depot or in some cases they are subcontracted outside. The depot managers have a sales function although at present business is 30 per cent below last year's level.

Three years ago a computer was installed and is the responsibility of the chief accountant. Existing applications include:

1. *Payroll* (gross-to-net pay). The gross pay is calculated manually from weekly time sheets.

2. *Customer billing* for the standard charge, variable rate, and operator time. Billing is monthly and the basic information is again captured from the coded time sheets.

3. *Sales ledger.*

4. *Purchase ledger and expenditure analysis.* The main costs are maintenance and repairs which are the responsibility of DPH.

5. *Contract costing* in which the actual costs incurred on each contract are compared with the actual revenue. The comparison is for the month and also cumulatively over the life of the contract.

6. *Management reports* which are mainly concerned with labour costs, maintenance costs, purchase of new plant, depreciation, plant utilisation and plant breakdowns.

In general, the users of the present systems are reasonably satisfied with them. However, the following criticisms have been made:

1. The payroll system 'only tackles the easy part of the problem – gross-to-net pay'. Five staff are still retained principally to calculate gross pay.

2. Credit control reports are inadequate. The average debt is currently fifteen weeks.

3. The contract costing reports need a good deal of interpretation by an experienced manager; the profit and loss figures as they appear in this computer report are often misleading.

A QUESTION OF PRIORITIES

The computer department has a number of projects planned and has asked you to indicate the priorities.

1. Sell spare computer time to associated companies in the Delia Group.
2. Preparation of trading accounts on the computer.
3. Analysis of profitability by depot.
4. Payroll build-up to gross from the time sheets. It would save a girl and tidy up the system.
5. Introduce improved debtor analysis to reduce the outstanding debt.
6. Build a corporate financial model to help monitor cash flows and to determine the best balance between 'contract' and 'spot hire'.
7. None of these.

Do not turn to page 42 yet. Stop and think through your solutions first.

CASE STUDY 2 – PERDITA PLASTICS

BACKGROUND

Perdita Plastics, turnover £7 million, has one main manufacturing plant and eight wholesale branch/warehouses across the country. Their products fall into two main categories: there are about 100 'standard' stock items which are stocked at all warehouses; and 'specials' made to customer contract stored in bulk at the appropriate warehouse, and called off by the customer as required.

Perdita has had a computer for a number of years and has accomplished more than most companies. It has some very able computer staff who have successfully introduced computer systems for invoicing, sales ledger, sales statistics, purchases, stock replenishment, costing, payroll and even a model of the distribution network.

THE NEXT STEP

The computer manager has now prepared a plan for the next stage. In essence the aim is to introduce 'on-line' order entry from the branches. This system would roughly double the cost of the existing computer because of the need for terminals in the branches, connecting telephone lines to the main computer, and a more powerful central computer. The benefits of the proposed system include:

daily analysis of orders from each branch

stock records for each branch held centrally with daily stock recording

central replenishment planning using the 'same day' stock figures (information available four days earlier than under the present system)

tighter control of depots where present systems are rather inaccurate and discipline poor

WHAT WOULD YOU DO?

The new computer system will cost an extra £40,000 a year to produce the benefits. There is also an additional factor. Although the staff have not said so, there is a real danger of losing them if you do not go ahead. They are highly skilled, competent, and the company would then run the risk of not being able to maintain their existing systems adequately.

What would you do?

1. Authorise the project to go ahead?
2. Reject the proposal and ask for a revised plan?
3. Decide to go ahead, but more slowly?

Make your decision, then read our analysis.

Here are our analyses.

DELIA SOLUTION

A question of objectives

When faced with a problem of deciding computer department priorities, it is essential to relate these priorities to the needs of the whole business. Looking at DPH, the major problem lies in marketing and sales. The level of business is 30 per cent below the level of last year so they have a lot of expensive plant and vehicles on their hands doing nothing. It is significant that there is not one sales or marketing analysis being produced by the computer, and only one of the proposals is even connected with marketing. Perhaps one reason is that the computer unit is identified with one department (in this case the accountants).

Now let us look at the suggested projects to see how they rank.

1. Selling spare computer time may look attractive but would be certain to lead to trouble. The clue is the lack of formal control procedures. Informal controls may be adequate for a small 'in-house' installation but will be totally inadequate for a service bureau operation.

2. Preparation of trading accounts on the computer is neither here nor there. It will merely replace an existing manual system with no significant benefits.

3. Analysis of profitability by depot looks more sensible and indeed it is surprising that it has not been done in the past. But before initiating a regular system to produce this analysis every month, why not do a single 'snapshot' manually to get the feel of the problem and to make sure it is worth while.

   In fact the results would be very interesting and would show that below a certain size, depots operate uneconomically. It turns out that they must be big enough to support full-time marketing and supervision if they are to be profitable.

4. Payroll build-up to gross is probably not very sensible and is unlikely to save any staff. The bulk of the work is computing

hours worked from the time sheets and applying quite complex rules to determine overtime, taking account of late clocking in. Not a very good computer application.

5. Introducing an improved debtor analysis in itself will do nothing to reduce the outstanding debt. What is required is somebody to be made responsible for following up bad debts and chasing customers to pay. This credit controller would be helped by faster (and possibly more frequent) billing.

6. Building a simple corporate model to compute the net balance between 'contract' and 'spot hire' in changing market conditions might be very useful for the future. Spot hire is very profitable when the plant is used above 70 per cent but carries a high risk when business is poor. Contract hire gives a lower rate of return but is less subject to market fluctuation.

VERDICT

The accountancy and computer staff need to be realigned so that their objectives are linked to the company objectives. In the immediate future their time should be deployed:

providing support for sales and marketing, e.g. by providing business trends by customer type, analysing depot profitability, balancing contract and spot hire. This support should be general systems support using the computer where appropriate.

re-appraising existing systems, e.g. to improve the debtor position, to rationalise the management reports, and to cut costs.

PERDITA SOLUTION

The way ahead

The dilemma facing the management of Perdita Plastics is one likely to be increasingly relevant to many organisations. On the one hand the cost of the proposals looks difficult to justify; on the other hand the company cannot risk losing its valued computer specialists. But let us look a little more carefully at that proposal.

1. Benefits of the proposed system One major benefit of the proposed system is the ability to analyse orders (rather than invoices) and so reduce the stock control delay by four days. This is probably a useful idea, but the same objective could be achieved by adding up the daily orders for each stock item at the depots. At the end of the day the 100 totals can be telephoned to the computer – a simple and cheap way of achieving the same result.

As for solving the depot problems, the computer is no panacea for deep-rooted management and labour problems. Computers, if you remember, prefer an orderly environment, not one where present systems are inaccurate and discipline poor.

2. Conversion problems The problems of converting the existing programs and systems from one type of computer to another are likely to keep the computer staff fully occupied for eighteen months at least. Is the upheaval worth while, and have the full costs of the conversion been considered?

3. Costs The brief to the problem suggested that the new system would cost an extra £40,000 p.a. However, as so often in real life, this was only the cost of the extra computer hardware. To this needs to be added:

the costs of converting existing programs to the new computer

the cost of developing appropriate 'on line' software

the cost of developing the new 'on line' application programs

the cost of data transmission

the cost of the additional hardware that always seems necessary (more core, another disc drive)

If we say, then, another £50,000–£100,000 to get the new system going, the proposition looks a good deal less attractive.

What should be done?

This analysis shows you cannot afford to go ahead with the project as it stands. The options open seem to be:

1. Thank the systems men warmly for their contribution to the company and help them to find new jobs. Recruit some 45-year-old programmers locally to maintain your systems. Rely on outside consultancy help in future if necessary.

2. Turn the best systems men into broader management services staff to help sort out the depots and to assist in developing more numerate management. Get rid of any surplus staff not required for maintenance.

3. Keep the team together by broadening their scope, as above, and selling spare capacity to other organisations

While any of these can work, they all raise problems. Can we get 45-year-old programmers? Will our best systems people leave anyway? What happens when the existing programs need rewriting in three to five years' time? Are the skills of the team easily marketable, and will we end up with more worries if we go for solution 3?

Perhaps the second solution is the most attractive, with our present knowledge.

THE COMPUTER EXPERT

A final word of warning. Be wary of computer experts and their impartial advice. A computer man is often much more concerned with techniques than with their application. For example, he is much more interested in the problems of implementing, say, 'Box-Jenkins forecasting' on a computer than in considering whether Box-Jenkins is the appropriate technique to use.

Secondly, he is a poor communicator and a worse listener. He will tend to ignore the ugly anomalies that exist in every business when they refuse to fit into his neat preconceptions. Challenge him and he will put up a smokescreen of incomprehensible jargon.

Thirdly, he is not over-concerned with schedules or budgets. He may draw them up in order to placate you, the manager, but he will retain the private conviction that his work is much too complex and subtle to be tied down in the mundane way that you require.

Fourthly, he is largely ignorant of the business that you are in. He thinks of himself primarily as a computer expert, and will regard your business problems as tiresome distractions that come between him and his real vocation.

Finally, he neglects the clerical systems that surround the computer. Left to himself, he will spend weeks redesigning a program so as to take a few minutes less on the computer, while leaving the users of the system to struggle with badly-designed forms and clumsy procedures.

Now this sketch is very much a caricature; that is to say that it might be a little difficult to find a computer 'expert' with *all* these vices. On the other hand, it might be equally difficult to find an expert untainted with *any* of them.

... a smokescreen of impenetrable jargon

SUMMARY

This chapter has shown that it is possible to distinguish between potentially successful computer applications and the obvious disasters. The main way is to identify jobs which have the necessary characteristics for easy computerisation and strong-mindedly reject the others no matter how desirable they may otherwise seem. The qualities needed are:

1. Information in the computer will be used repeatedly
2. The application in question helps to link corporate activities
3. Information and instructions for the computer will need infrequent change
4. Corporate procedures are clear and comprehensible
5. Managers using the computer are keen and involved
6. The system to be replaced is not an irredeemable mess
7. Installing a computer will yield identifiable net cash savings

If the projected application lacks several of these characteristics it will be a disruptive drain on management and money. But a lot can be done to make jobs more systematic and computer-suitable – sometimes that can mean the computer is no longer required.

Chapter 3

The Sort of Work Computers Are Used For

Having looked at the ways to spot likely applications for computerisation in the previous chapter, we shall now take a brief look at three main areas where computers are currently being used. All three are complex subjects so this chapter is fairly heavy with information. We do not suggest that you skip it because it gives a practical background to set Chapters 4 and 5 in perspective, but you may like to return to it again later.

First we shall look at data processing to see how a system is designed; and to show the sort of thinking and analysis that must be done before a computer is installed – it is unbelievably difficult afterwards. This area is basically the clerical drudgery which is indispensable in all organisations – boring but fundamental.

A second area is management information which still remains difficult and controversial. Partly this is because of the conflict of two instinctive views: one is that this is just the area computers were invented for and should be good at (thus ignoring the complexity of the information and hence the difficulty of getting it into and out of the machine); and the other view that says management is an art which cannot be mechanised (thus forgetting how much of the work is routine or could at least be systematised).

The important thing here is to identify the problem before the solution – it is amazing how often otherwise sane people do it the other way about. Remember the consultancy aphorism – the solution in search of problems approach has enjoyed general failure. Victor Borge put the same point in his story of an uncle who, doing medical research, found a cure for which there was no known disease. Unfortunately his wife caught the cure and died.

Finally we look at on-line computer systems to show an approach which is becoming popular. This helps management work in real-time (computer jargon for instant response) and is therefore frequently used for corporate planning.

A. DATA PROCESSING

Though much of this book has talked about business, this sort of work is applicable to just about any sort of organisation. Examples range from Royal Army Pay Corps records to supermarket stock control, from credit card billing to an on-line savings bank system, from engineering production scheduling to civil engineering estimates. So the applications are varied and extensive. Whether any particular organisation opts to put distribution control or payroll on to a computer will depend on its circumstances and how the application rates on suitability criteria such as those of Chapter 2.

It would obviously be impossible to list all possibilities with problems and approaches, so we have taken the example of stock control and invoicing because it has wide applicability and is often used.

The example is of 'pre-despatch' in which stock control and invoicing are carried out before the goods are despatched.

THE MANUAL SYSTEM

1. Orders received from customers are transcribed on to a standard order form.

2. Orders from different branches of the same customer are brought together because large customers normally prefer one summarised invoice. They may also receive a bulk discount.

3. Stock availability for each item ordered is checked on stock cards and the balances there reduced by the numbers ordered. Items are marked 'To follow' if no stock is available.

   Price, code and full description are added from the stock cards to the order form.

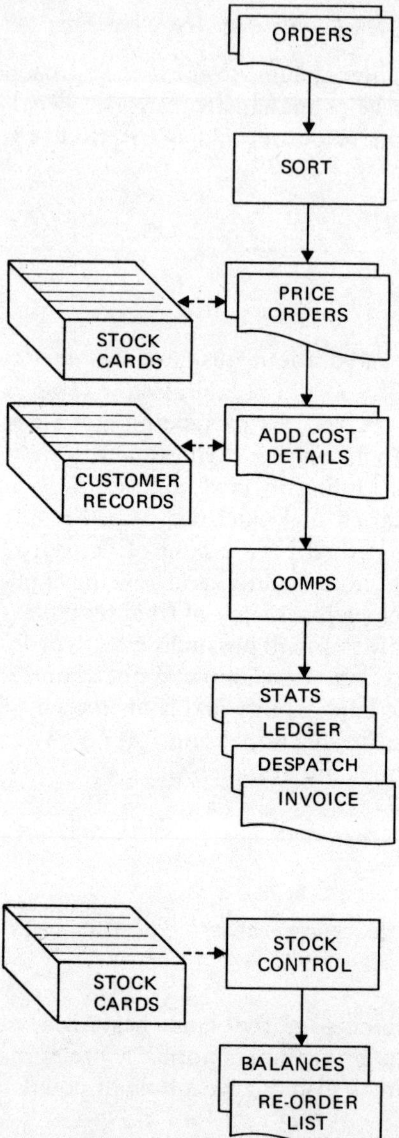

1. Orders received from customer.
2. Sort orders from the same customer together.
3. Look up stock balances for items ordered. Check stock is available, record issues. Price and code items, write out new stock balances.
4. Look up customer record. Add discount rate, special delivery instructions and codes (representative, sales area, customer class).
5. Extend invoice items and total.
6. Type invoice set, including: Invoice, Despatch Note, Sales Ledger copy, Statistics copy.
7. At the end of the day scan stock cards. Write out stock balances and Re-order list.

FIG. 6 Stock Control and Invoicing – Manually

The flowchart shows the step-by-step operations which might be carried out during a clerical invoicing procedure. The procedure is known as 'pre-despatch' as the stock control is carried out before the Invoice and Despatch note, which are prepared together. Note that checking procedures are not shown, nor the work required to keep the stock cards and customer records up to date.

4. The customer record card is now referred to for discount rates, special delivery instructions and codes – account number, rep code, area code, customer class, etc. These codes are also added to the order form.

5. The order items are extended and the total value calculated by machine or by comptometer operator.

6. The order now contains all the details necessary for the invoice with four copies (invoice, despatch note, sales ledger copy and statistics copy) all typed at the same time.

7. At the end of the day the stock cards are analysed to produce a list of stock balances and a list of items to be reordered. The decision to reorder is taken if the balance falls below a preset level, recalculated periodically.

This process can be transferred to a computer, but the computer must be told precisely the rules for such things as:

the stock control system to be adopted
the level of customer service
how to allocate insufficient stock
the priorities for satisfying 'back orders' when stock does become available
how to reconcile physical stock discrepancies
how to code stock items
how to code customers
how to guard against coding errors
how to keep customer files up to date
pricing policy and discount structure
how to handle credits and show them in sales analyses
how to apply value added tax and what flexibility to allow for future government tax changes

The computer we will use consists of:

Central processing unit
Card reader
Printer
Five magnetic tape drives

Customer Order Ref.	Sales Area	Rep.	Customer Class	Account No.	Order No. Date:

Invoice address:	Delivery address:
Delivery instructions:	Delivery date:

Qty	Description	Code	VAT rate	Price		Value	
				£	p	£	p
					TOTAL		
					VAT		
					TOTAL DUE		

FIG. 7 Specimen Invoice – Manual System

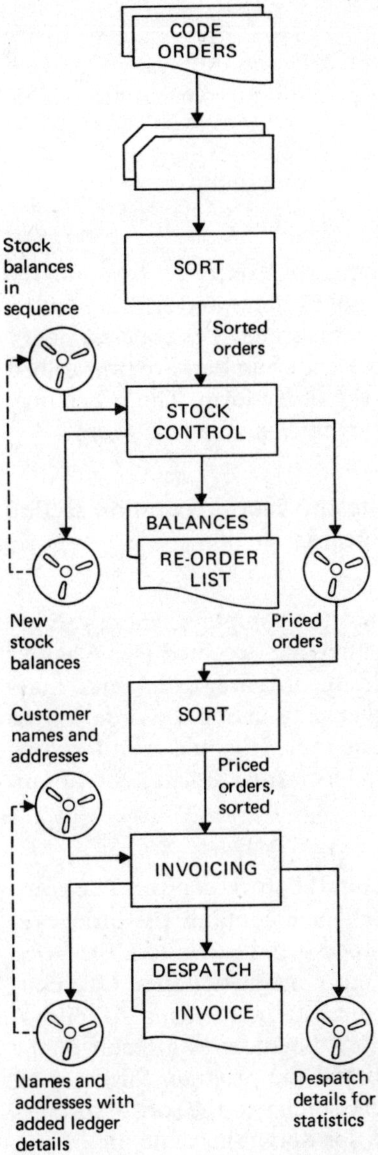

1. Orders received from customers.
   Add customer code and item codes.

2. Punch and verify one card per item.

3. Read cards on to magnetic tape.
   Sort items to stock code sequence.

4. Read order items in turn.
   Read corresponding stock balance.
   Check stock is available, record issues, price items.
   Write out new stock balances on to tape.
   Print stock balances and re-order list.
   Write out priced orders to tape for invoicing.

5. Sort priced items to customer sequence.

6. Read orders in turn.
   Read corresponding customer record.
   Add discount rate, delivery instructions and codes (representative, sales area, customer class).
   Extend and total.
   Print Invoice and Despatch Note.
   Write out new customer file with added ledger details.
   Write out despatch details for statistical analysis.

FIG. 8 Stock Control and Invoicing – Magnetic Tape

This flowchart shows how a computer with magnetic tape peripherals might be used for the stock control and invoicing job described in figure 6. Note that the programs required to check the input for validity, to keep the stock file up-to-date and to keep the customer file up-to-date are not shown.

We will only be able to use four tape drives in our system because the fifth holds the computer programs, and is not normally available for other work.

THE COMPUTER SYSTEM (MAGNETIC TAPE)

1. Orders are received from customers as before, but this time the computer identifies customers not by name and address but by account number and identifies stock items by code numbers. So the account number and stock code numbers are transcribed from printed code lists on to the order form. The order may also be transcribed at this stage on to a standard form.

2. Batches of orders are passed to the data preparation section where they are punched on to cards.

3. The punched cards are read into the computer where validity checks are carried out before they are accepted (see Chapter 6, page 144). The accepted order records are sorted on to magnetic tape into *stock code* sequence to match the order of the stock balances held on magnetic tape. It would take too long (winding the tape backwards and forwards) to find items at random.

4. The next computer run carries out the stock control. The computer reads two magnetic tapes – one contains the orders received, the other the stock balances – and carries out the stock recording and writes out two more magnetic tapes. One contains the priced orders with signals to mark items 'to follow'. The other contains the new stock balances as a result of the transactions. The process used and the program for carrying out this computer run looks very similar to the sort of instructions you would give to a clerk for doing the same job, if you told him the job in a methodical way.

   Some of the instructions a programmer might use are shown in Figure 9. The programming 'language' used is known as COBOL (COmmon Business Oriented Language) – a widely used programming language for business applications.

In addition to carrying out stock recording the computer prints a re-order list for those items whose stock balance has fallen below the re-order level.

5. The orders have been priced and stock availability checked, but the orders are still in stock number sequence. The next step is to sort them into customer account number sequence because all items ordered by the same customer outlet need to be

```
...
STEP-A.
  READ ORDER-FILE.
STEP-B1.
  READ STOCK-FILE.
STEP-B2.
  IF CODE OF ORDER-ITEM EQUALS CODE OF STOCK-RECORD GO TO STEP-C.
  IF CODE OF ORDER-ITEM IS LESS THAN CODE OF STOCK-RECORD GO TO STEP-E.
STEP-C.
  IF STOCK-BALANCE IS LESS THAN ORDER-QTY GO TO SHORTAGE-ROUTINE.
  SUBTRACT ORDER-QTY FROM STOCK-BALANCE.
  MOVE PRICE OF STOCK-RECORD TO PRICE OF ORDER-ITEM.
STEP-D.
  PERFORM ORDER-ITEM-PRINT.
  READ ORDER-FILE.
  GO TO STEP-B2.
STEP-E.
  WRITE STOCK-RECORD-OUT.
  GO TO STEP-B1.
...
```

FIG. 9 Part of COBOL Program for Stock Recording

This figure shows some of the instructions in a program for stock recording. The programming language used is COBOL. Only some of the necessary instructions are shown. For example the error routines are omitted. One such error would arise if no stock record were found for one of the order items – perhaps a code was entered incorrectly. Typically this program when complete would consist of 500–1000 instructions.

despatched and invoiced together, and because the customer details are already on magnetic tape in account number sequence.

6. The final invoicing run is similar to the stock control run. The computer reads two magnetic tapes; one contains the priced orders, the other the customer details. The first order item is read and the corresponding customer located. The customer name and address is read and printed out at the top of the combined invoice and despatch note. Then each item ordered is printed with its value and the values accumulated. When all the items have been printed the invoice total is printed at the foot of the page after allowing the appropriate discounts.

   Two new magnetic tapes are written during the operation. The first contains the customer details complete with the invoice total, which is needed for end of month statements. The second contains the original customer order items to which analysis codes (rep, sales area, customer class) have been added and will be used for preparing sales statistics and management reports.

The computer procedures described follow the manual procedures fairly closely. There are two main differences:

1. Computers process very exactly. This makes it difficult for them to recognise that I. S. Rossini of 1 High Street is the same man as Ibrahim Sean Rossini, The Larches, High St. To get over the problem all input items must be coded. The computer then recognises them and matches them by their code.

2. Orders had first to be sorted to stock sequence for the stock control, then to customer sequence for the invoicing. These sortings were necessary because the files were held on magnetic tape, and looking up items at random on magnetic tape is very time-consuming.

Using a computer with magnetic disc storage as well as magnetic tapes allows the processing to be done slightly differently. As we shall see, this may have its advantages.

MAGNETIC DISC SYSTEM

The computer we will use this time consists of:

Central processing unit
Card reader
Printer
Three magnetic tape drives
Three magnetic disc drives

There is a flowchart showing the system using this computer in Figure 10.

Using this 'random access' system, orders for the same customer

... looking up items at random on magnetic tape is very time-consuming

stay together and stock control and invoicing is carried out in one computer run. The computer reads the sorted orders from magnetic tape, the customer names and addresses from a second magnetic tape, and the stock balances from magnetic discs.

In most cases it is not important to look at the whole of the customer order when checking that stock is available (the tape system sorted apart each item the customer ordered), but imagine the situation where customers stipulate they will not accept part deliveries. You would need to check that stock is available for all items before preparing the invoice, otherwise stock may be tied up which might complete another customer's order. In this type of situation some form of random access (e.g. discs) is essential.

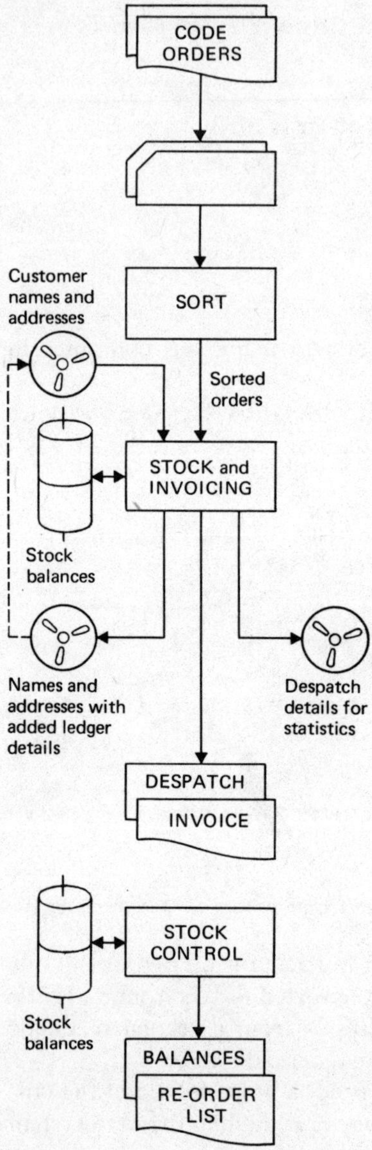

1. Orders received from customers.
   Add customer code and item codes.

2. Punch and verify one card per item.

3. Read orders on to magnetic tape.
   Sort orders to customer sequence.

4. Read orders in turn.
   Look up stock records on disc.
   Check stock is available, record issues.
   Price items. Write out new stock balances.
   Read customer record.
   Add discount rate, delivery instructions, and codes (representative, sales area, customer class).
   Extend and total.
   Print invoice and despatch note.
   Write out new customer record with sales ledger details.
   Write despatch details to tape for statistical analysis.

5. At the end of the day scan the stock records.
   Print stock balances and re-order list.

FIG. 10 Stock Control and Invoicing – Magnetic Disc and Tape
The flowchart shows how the stock control and invoicing job described in figures 6 and 8 might be carried out using a computer with magnetic disc and tape peripherals. Note that the programs required to check the input for validity are not shown, nor the programs to keep the stock file and the customer file up-to-date.

On magnetic tape, each stock record after being processed was written on to a new tape. The old tape was only 'read' and remains unaffected by the processing. This old tape is known as the 'father' of the newly created 'son'. For security a copy of the 'grandfather' is retained so that the job can be re-run should any error be subsequently detected.

Using magnetic discs, a completely new disc is not normally created – the old record is merely over-written if it is changed. The reason for this is that records are normally looked up at random, some perhaps several times, others not at all; on magnetic tape each record is read once and in sequence.

Security using discs is reduced because the original record is destroyed when over-written. To allow the possibility of re-running, the disc file must be copied on to another disc or on to a tape (cheaper) at the end of the day. Using discs, one must devise other methods of ensuring security against error and cope with the increased complexity of computer 'housekeeping'. For instance, should room be left for a new stock item to be added to the middle of the file and waste space, or should there be an 'overflow' area? But having an overflow area means the file soon gets into quite a mess and needs to be cleaned up. In practice a combination of the two methods is used with about 10 per cent space left for new items and 'overflow' areas used where this is not enough.

B. MANAGEMENT INFORMATION SYSTEMS

We have already pointed out the dangers of investing in computers without a clear idea of the benefits to be obtained. All too often the computer justification depends largely on claimed intangible benefits. One of the most seductive of these intangibles is management information. Seductive because of the emotive arguments that can be employed. For example:

> 'Timely management information is essential to the running of the organisation in today's competitive business environment.'

> 'The use of a computer puts us in a position to produce a vast number and variety of management reports.'

'How can we put a price on the provision of this essential information?'

'The right information at the right time may make all the difference between success and failure in our business.'

So where is the fallacy? Well, management information is a vague and slippery term that has never been properly defined. It can mean merely the extra computer benefit we cannot pin down (a sort of balancing item), or essential sales statistics, or it can be a blanket word for all the unfocused feelings that executives would be more effective if they got more figures (forgetting that when they do get them they often cannot or do not use them).

Some of the factors which have inhibited the development of an effective MIS are:

Users have failed to establish what the management information is for and how it will be used.

People have become fascinated with the technology and hence have disregarded cheaper methods of processing information.

The information that can reasonably be found in a computer system is limited – the information that really matters for the running of a business is often not there, and cannot be.

Proposals for systems have often ignored cost/benefit calculations and where even a cursory attempt has been made, the cost has been minimised and the benefit exaggerated.

Men are flexible, intuitive, can adapt to uncertainty and imprecision; the computer is almost the exact opposite and so can be very difficult to use.

Computer specialists have often designed systems in ignorance of true management problems, and they have frequently been inadequately controlled.

So even if we do determine the information managers need we must still check that the computer is the best way of producing it. As we shall see later, the computer does have a role but it is a less glamorous one than is commonly imagined.

It is probable that the more important a management decision is, the higher the risk it carries and the more far-reaching the outcome, the less likely it is that the information for that decision will be found in the computer system. So a huge investment in computer hardware and in the development of computer 'data bases' specifically for management information is in many cases irrelevant to the needs of the business.

Notice that we distinguish here between computers used for management information and computers used for data processing – i.e. mechanising the operating systems. The point is that to make best use of your computer, the systems and files should be designed with data processing in mind rather than the provision of management information.

BACKGROUND TO MIS

The references to management information have occurred in volume only since the advent of computers. Originally the intention was that all the operational running of the business would be integrated with the information flow into a giant computer complex. Orders would be passed into the system, which would automatically print invoices, carry out stock control, re-order from the factory, carry out production planning and control, produce the payroll and management accounts and so on. Middle management would become a dying race and the senior managers would sit back feeding the system with economic and seasonal trends from time to time.

Early attempts to mechanise the operating systems on computers hit difficulties whenever there existed any degree of management discretion in decision-making. Far from being reduced, middle management grew new technical limbs (statisticians, operational researchers, financial analysts, etc.).

Then people realised that computer systems could not do it all. Many operations would continue to be done by clerical staff and many decisions would be required from managers. There remained, however, the desirability of 'integrating' separate operations; instead of holding two customer name and address files (one for invoicing, one for sales ledger), one would be sufficient. The idea of a 'common data base' was born. This data base would hold both current and historical information and be available for management interrogation.

Some companies are spending over £1m. a year automating their systems and have been successful in areas with limited discretion. Not content with this, however, some companies have gone on investing in hardware and people to develop a common data base that would enable them to answer almost any enquiry. This has proved expensive and consistently unsuccessful.

If we accept that the operating system is not really the same as the management information system, many present-day computers are financially unjustifiable.

INFORMATION FOR DECISION-MAKING

Many people still associate MIS with computers but there is no necessary connection. It is perhaps wiser to start at the other end; it is more sensible to ask first what the purpose is of management information. It is then immediately obvious that information is itself valueless – what is important is the decision made with the information.

This then provides the starting point. Any other approach is like building a road before knowing where you want to go. There are several ways of tackling the problem even from this angle, but the most useful one we have found is to start by identifying the key decision areas of a manager's job. Then the information necessary to make those decisions is essential.

A fundamental management process is making decisions, for which managers need specific information about the organisation and its external environment. It is the function of a management information system to provide this information.

Notice that this definition does not say what an MIS is – it says what it does. The definition also points the way towards a framework for management information, based on decisions.

Few managers, however, take their decisions in isolation. Their individual decisions should collectively contribute to overall company objectives. Perhaps this sounds obvious, but **many executives do not have a clear idea of what is expected of them.**

In one study carried out in California a number of managers were asked to state the ten most important features of their job by which they were judged. These managers' superiors were then asked, separately, to assess the ten most important features they used to judge their subordinate manager's performance. Subsequent comparison showed that the boss and his subordinate had very different views of the subordinate's job.

This study suggests that it is prudent to start at the top of the business. **Set clear objectives for the business as a whole and then examine the decision areas of managers within this framework. There is no point in giving managers information to do the wrong job better.**

THREE LEVELS OF DECISIONS

To identify the different decision areas it is helpful to look separately for the three decision levels:

1. Strategic policy decisions: affecting the medium- and long-term plans for the business.

2. Tactical planning decisions: how best to achieve the strategic policy in the short term.

3. Operational control decisions: to implement plans to run the enterprise on a day-to-day basis.

Information for *strategic policy decisions* is required mainly to evaluate alternative company strategies, and to minimise risks. The information required tends to be unpredictable, of low volume and often external to business. It is therefore highly unlikely that this kind of information can ever be provided from the in-house computer. The role of the computer at this level is more likely to be in the evaluation of alternative strategies using computer models.

Information for making *tactical decisions* is required in areas such as the best use of the available resources to achieve company objectives (e.g. what stock control systems should be introduced for various product categories); calculating standards of performance to be achieved (e.g. to supply 98 per cent ± 1 per cent of customer orders from stock over any three-month period, thus balancing the cost of increasing stock against the cost of losing customers).

The main characteristic of this information is that it is project-orientated – because most planning is irregular. For example you do not regularly replan your stock control system but take action when something goes wrong. Because the information is needed irregularly and often at long intervals, the computer tends not to be suitable. What is required is a capacity to answer *ad hoc* queries, either by interrogating computer files or by using clerical staff.

Information for *operational control* is concerned with significant deviations from plan. For example, customer service falling below 97 per cent would be highlighted for management investigation. The preparation of this type of exception report is well suited to computer systems.

This analysis of information characteristics confirms the previous chapter. The computer is best suited to the repetitive, low risk, predictable work associated with operational control and the automation of operational procedures. When decisions move to strategic level, only some of the important information can ever come from the computer system.

IMPROVING THE MIS

All organisations already have an MIS, so to be realistic we must aim to *improve* what exists rather than to ignore it. In other words there is no point in saying, as did the joke Irishman, 'If I were going there sorr, I wouldn't start from here.'

So where to begin? We suggest that an overall plan for MIS improvement should be prepared and reviewed annually with a planning horizon typically stretching ahead five years. Within the overall plan we have found useful four major lines of attack.

1. *Exploit existing systems*

Major improvements take years, but improving existing systems can achieve measurable improvements in a relatively short time. One way of starting is to pinpoint problem areas and agree a set of priorities for improvement.

Here are some examples where short-term action was taken to improve existing systems:

> One hire purchase company engaged a press-cutting service to provide highly relevant and much-needed information. This information was readily available but they had not been receiving it.

Another company, in the food business, wrote a new computer program to sort invoices into branch within customer sequence, before they were printed. Previously five girls had been required to sort and summarise the computer-produced invoices manually.

A manufacturing company was spending over £100,000 a year, buying computer time, above the cost of their own computer (which was on three shifts). It bought and installed another computer, secondhand, for only £60,000.

A pharmaceutical company with a high customer debt was able to use its computer to produce monthly an aged debt analysis. Coupled with an aggressive follow-up policy, the average debt was reduced by twenty days.

These examples show that organisations develop blind spots. A periodic review can expose a number of areas where tangible benefits can be achieved. When looking for benefits it is useful to consider simplifying existing clerical procedures as well as exploiting the computer.

Simplifying existing clerical procedures is a traditional O & M area and it is usually possible to 'save' 20 per cent – getting the same work done by fewer staff or allowing the same staff to carry out more work. It is achieved by method study, work measurement and planning and control.

Where computers are in use there is considerable interaction between clerical and computer procedures and this is an area susceptible to major improvement in most organisations.

2. *Establish an MIS framework*

We have seen that it is difficult for managers to identify their real information needs without priorities and a framework. This means identifying the Key Decision Areas (KDAs) within the business and getting agreement both with the manager and his boss on the subordinate's KDAs. But before identifying the key decision areas for individual managers one must look at the business as a whole for three reasons:

The managers' efforts must be directed towards common objectives.

The existing organisation structure may be unsuitable and may not reflect the decision-making needs of the business.

Organisation structures are more likely to change than the basic decision-making needs in the major fundamental areas of the business.

In one distribution company we found the main source of business was a declining market – at the present rate of decline it would be out of business within seven years. The fundamental task was to gather external information to assist this company to establish where they wished to be in five years' time; and to set clear company objectives.

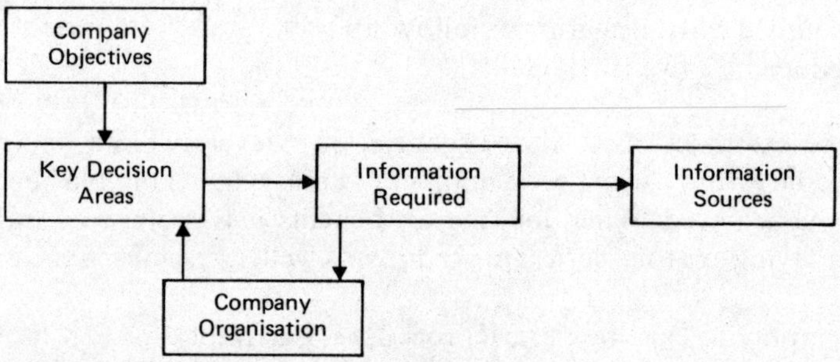

FIG. 11 Company Objectives

Company objectives are more permanent than the existing organisation. In developing an information system it is thus appropriate to go from Objectives to Key Decision Areas to Information Required and to establish Information Sources and then to relate requirements to the organisation.

Once objectives have been agreed, it is possible to identify six or seven key decision areas in each function – such as sales, marketing, stock control, production planning, production control, purchasing, accounts and distribution.

From the key decision areas it is possible to identify the information needed in broad categories. A comparison of the information needed with the existing sources of information will tend to reveal the gaps – and to some extent the duplication. The most common gaps lie in both external information and planning information which is, by its nature, more unpredictable and more difficult to formalise.

The next step is to compare the decision analysis with the existing organisation. It is helpful to use here the decision influence grid illustrated in Figure 12.

'Organisation' is a complex area and it can be hard to decide whether to leave the existing organisation, with its possibly sub-optimal decision-making ability, or to have an organisational upheaval. Once this decision is taken, detailed responsibility can be agreed for the key decision areas. This is an operation which requires the close co-operation of each manager and his boss.

It is probable that some such analysis should be carried out every couple of years. The organisation is not static nor are the objectives of the business, and the key decision areas may change their emphasis. The main point is that the analysis starts at the top of the business and that managers must clearly understand their de-

	Sales Functior KDAs	Marketing Function KDAs	Order Processing KDAs
Sales Manager			
Marketing Manager			
Office Manager			
Chief Accountant			

FIG. 12 Decision Influence Grid
The Decision Influence Grid is used to identify which managers take major responsibility for the Key Decision Areas.

cision-making responsibilities. It is not a question of hiring a few computer men and leaving them to get on with it.

3. *Rationalise management reports*
Most formal reporting systems rely upon paperwork, have evolved over a period of time and have developed a number of inadequacies. If you ask any manager what is wrong, his reply may be:

> 'I get *too much* information and find it difficult to sort out the relevant facts.'
>
> 'Although I get too much information, what I get is still inadequate for many purposes. There is *insufficient relevant* information.'
>
> 'Many of my reports are *too late* for my needs.'

Customer Service

What levels of customer service should we achieve?

deliveries from stock

speed of order processing and despatch

How can we further improve relations with our key customers (the 20 per cent who account for 80 per cent of the business)?

What procedure is required for handling customer complaints?

Profitability

How can sales profitability be improved?

What pricing and discount structure should we adopt?

Sales Forecasts

How can the accuracy of sales forecasts be improved?

How can sales best be increased by 25 per cent over the next three years?

Control

How should sales force control be exercised?

What systems of credit control do we need?

FIG. 13 Examples of Key Decision Areas for a Sales Manager

The key decision areas are not meant to be exhaustive, nor will these KDAs be valid for every sales manager. The key decision areas will depend on the problems of the organisation and the pressures on the individual managers.

PLANNING DECISIONS

1. The use of resources
2. Standards of performance
3. To delegate
4. New projects
5. For profit
6. To improve weaknesses
7. Staff development

CONTROLLING DECISIONS

1. Resources
2. Costs
3. Waste
4. Quality
5. Projects

FIG. 14 Check List for Identifying Key Decision Areas

This figure may be useful as a check list when considering your key decision areas. It is often helpful to express the decision area in the form of a question. For example, 'What stock control systems should we employ?'

'Many reports are both *too accurate* – with figures calculated to two places of decimals – and yet *inaccurate* – the wrong figures are put in the wrong places.'

It is easier to add a new report than to scrap an old one. The information passed out is often based on what is available and what was once asked for in the distant past by the previous manager but three. It is easier to circulate an extra copy than to remove one and distortions creep in, unless the system is continually under review.

There is clearly considerable scope for improvement in most organisations. An executive who reduced his regular management reports from 150 per month down to eight was a fairly extreme case, but you would expect to reduce the number of management reports by up to 50 per cent.

In appraising management reports the first test is for *relevance*. What is the worst that could happen if you never saw it again? Such a check through all reports will quickly show large areas of redundant information and even completely redundant reports. Compare the result with your key decision areas – mainly the operational control key decision areas. Your purpose is to ensure that the reports you get reflect the priorities implicit in your key decision areas.

The second test is for *consistency and accuracy*. Are the figures in all your reports consistent in units, time-scales and adding up to the same figures in the bottom right-hand corner? Are the figures sufficiently accurate for the purpose for which they are to be used? Are they soundly based? For example, on what basis are overheads allocated; is this basis sensible for the use that is to be made of the figures?

The third test is for *comparative figures*. Almost all regular reports are required for management control; and if control is to be exercised there must be comparative figures to signify exceptions and to detect trends. If we are to manage by exception it is necessary both to set clear objectives at the planning stage and also to define the amount we are prepared to deviate from these objectives.

The fourth test is for *level of detail*. The reports should contain those key factors which cover 80 per cent or so of the problem areas. As a guide, **you need enough information to be sure subordinates are doing their job; but not so much that you could do their job for them.** Be realistic about what you can achieve (if it is only feasible to take action on ten product groups in any month, why be told about more?), but make sure more detail is available on call. Go for simple indicators, graphs, histograms, where they can show significant deviations more clearly. And check that you can identify the crucial factors when things start to go wrong – you do not want too many 'red lights' coming on at once without some guide to their significance.

The fifth test is for *frequency*. Many existing reports are geared to the accounting cycle without regard to the demands of the business. The questions to ask when determining frequency are: How serious might the situation get if corrective action is not taken? How quickly could it get out of control? What is the practicable rate of change in management policy? Too frequent measurements give an undesirable 'flicker' (daily sales figures?); too slow or infrequent measurements cause delay in taking corrective action. Finally, be prepared to change the frequency to reflect the changing needs of the business.

Once this type of analysis has been carried out it is possible to design improved reporting systems. The steps required to improve the reporting system are:

1. Establish the key decision areas (KDAs) within each function and for each decision-taking manager.

2. Review all existing management reports, testing them for relevance, consistency and accuracy; ensure that there are comparative figures available, that there is the right level of detail, and that they are at the right frequency.

3. Compare existing reports with the KDAs: establish what is irrelevant, what additional information is required, its source and presentation.

4. Design the new reporting system taking into account the possibility of using both clerical and computer processing.

5. Periodically review the reporting system.

4. *Explore strategic problems*

Perhaps the most fundamental concept for successful planning is the idea of exploring alternative solutions. Evaluating alternatives tends to improve all the possible solutions considered, because you will trade one off against the other and learn more about your problem as you do so.

Organisations often do not formulate their objectives explicitly or do so with insufficient information and without serious consideration of different objectives.

We have already mentioned the company which was operating (very efficiently) in a declining market. The primary task of top manage-

```
YOU MAY INPUT ADJUSTMENTS TO THE EXPECTED
SALES AND STOCK FOR EACH OF YOUR  4    PRODUCT GROUPS;
AND FOR ADMIN,PRODN AND DEBTORS COSTS IN TOTAL.
ADJUSTMENTS ARE.EXPRESSED AS A PERCENT CHANGE (+OR-)
FROM THE ORIGINAL FIGURES.  0 MEANS NO CHANGE.

INPUT CHANGES TO SALES,STOCK
     SPARE-MFD? +10,-20
     SPARES-BO? +10,-10
     ACCES-MFD? +50,-20
     ACCESS-BO? +50,-20

INPUT TOTAL CHANGES TO ADMIN,PRODN,DEBTORS? -10,-5,-20

                  MOTOR COMPONENTS - CONTRIBUTION ANALYSIS


TYPE 1 IF YOU WISH TO SEE TOTALS ONLY?1


                 SPARE-MFD    SPARES-BO    ACCES-MFD    ACCESS-BO      TOTALS

CONTRIBUTION        1195           275           86          137         1693
CON.PER UNIT        0.52          0.28         0.38         0.38         0.44

LIQUIDITY            280            66          -50          -67          230


TOTAL CONTRIBUTION      1692.76
FIXED COSTS             1220.00
NET PROFIT               472.76
PROFIT/SALES %             6.91
IMPROVED LIQUIDITY       229.50
```

FIG. 15 Making Adjustments to the Company Model

This figure shows the results of increasing sales (10 per cent for spares; 50 per cent for accessories), reducing stock, and attacking the administration, production and debtor costs. The result is an increased contribution to 1693 and a particular improvement in the profitability of the manufactured spares.

ment was to identify certain key strategic questions that had to be answered, then set up an *ad hoc* data gathering system to help explore the alternative courses of action.

A carpet manufacturer had increased in size by 50 per cent over the previous five years and had set a goal of another increase of 50 per cent during the next five years. After two years they found themselves in serious financial trouble due to a shortage of cash – having expanded too fast for their resources. They had failed to gather all the available information and to use it to explore the implications of alternative strategic policies.

Evaluating alternative courses of action implies some form of simulation of the future. Figure 15 shows a company model constructed on a computer.

While it is not always necessary or even desirable to use a computer for all models, the advent of timesharing computer terminals has made it easy to use one. Senior managers, with the assistance of a statistician or financial analyst, can construct models to simulate a number of different aspects of the business (such as cash flow, contribution by divisions or product groups, use of critical resources). The decisions that follow this type of evaluation will in almost every case be substantially better than the 'rule of thumb' decision.

One large American food company acquired considerable expertise in the use of mathematical models to support decision-making. It started by attempting to construct a large-scale comprehensive corporate model but had to abandon it on grounds of complexity. It now uses a series of small models related to individual product/markets to predict product performance and hence to reduce risk in the launching of new products. Models are currently used as a routine aid to decisions at senior and middle management levels, and the president of the corporation personally builds some models. But it has been found that surprisingly little of the information for these models tends to come from the computer system.

Although we are advocating that managers should become more familiar with models and computer terminals, we do not seriously envisage that every senior executive shall have a terminal on his desk. Senior managers rarely take important decisions quickly and the higher the risk the more thought should go into the decision. Any senior manager who is required to take repetitive decisions rapidly should seriously consider specifying the rules in detail and then delegating the job. Otherwise the only realistic way of running the business would be to have three chief executives, working in shifts, ready for instantaneous decision-making.

ORGANISING FOR AN MIS

There are two major phases in implementing an improved MIS. The first is analytical – deciding what information managers need. The second phase is design – how best to achieve it. The second phase of design is the better understood area and a good systems team should be able to cope with the problem. It is the analytical phase which presents the difficulty. Both company objectives and company organisation must be questioned before beginning the design phase of an MIS. It may also be necessary to educate managers to use their information more effectively.

Outside help may be required because it is often easier for an outsider to question company practice and to identify areas of weakness. In addition, an outsider can talk more frankly to senior management. Outside help is often necessary to bring about change. So an internal project team could be supplemented or led by the outsider. In this way the lessons learned are not lost to the organisation. The project team must be of very high calibre – men who will be missed when they are seconded from their departments.

We do not of course suggest that the information team should usurp the role of senior management. But we are all resistant to change and if the team members just accept what they are told their impact on the firm will be negligible. Using the right team the impact can be considerable.

SUMMARY

Although there is no necessary connection, computers do have a contribution to MIS, because larger organisations have major problems with management information, and these firms often use computers.

Information is required for management decisions and it is helpful to look for three broad levels of decision:

Strategic policy decisions

Tactical planning decisions

Operational control decisions

The information required for strategic decisions tends to be unpredictable, of low volume, often unformalised and to a large extent external to the business. At the other extreme the information for operational control is predictable, high volume, very formalised and almost entirely internal to the business.

Designing a comprehensive MIS for an organisation is almost bound to lead to expensive failure. The right approach is to accept that the organisation already has an MIS and the objective must be to improve it. We have found four ways of improving an MIS:

Exploit existing systems, going for short-term benefits and a solution to persistent problem areas

Establish an MIS framework, using the analysis of key decision areas

Rationalise management reports, and set up a system for answering *ad hoc* requests

Explore strategic problems using mathematical models and evaluating alternative solutions

C. ON-LINE COMPUTERS AND TIMESHARING SYSTEMS

ENQUIRY SYSTEMS

In general there are 'instant' response and delayed response enquiry systems. The best known examples of 'instant' response are the airline seat reservation systems. With the volume of business generated by large airlines, it would be difficult to keep up-to-the-minute records of seat availability without using computers. On heavily booked flights computers can help to sell more tickets because the records are always up to date, and the exact position of bookings and cancellations can be discovered from the ticket desks by dialling up the computer. But the cost of these real-time, 'on-line', 'instant response' computer systems can be immense.

Delayed response enquiries are cheaper. If you want to know the state of a customer account or the quantities of product A sold per week for the last ten weeks in each region, then (assuming the information is already in the computer) there are two ways of digging out the answers.

The first is often the more practical, although less glamorous. Use the computer to print out periodic reference reports from which clerical staff abstract the answers to these *ad hoc* questions. This approach is the best when the pattern of questions is difficult to predict. Writing a special computer program to answer random enquiries can be very uneconomic.

On the other hand, if the pattern of enquiries is well known, it may be possible to write an economical enquiry program. One way of doing this is to accumulate all enquiries that arrive during the morning and process them as a batch at, say, midday. If you are prepared to wait a few hours for your answers, the work can be fitted into existing computer schedules with the minimum disruption.

All this makes depressing reading if your problem is maintaining stock records 'up to the minute'. On the one hand, instant response is too expensive, but waiting an hour for an answer is too long. But there are other possibilities:

1. In stock control, get the computer to print two lists overnight; one of items which are definitely out of stock, the other of items which are likely to go out of stock before the next computer run. To answer queries, all that is required is to record stock movements for the 'at risk' items.

2. Don't despair of using an on-line computer. There is a growing small computer industry. Small computers which are dedicated to, say, stock control and invoicing, are becoming more widely available. These computers typically consist of a small central processing unit, a magnetic disc to store stock items, and electric typewriters for entering order quantities and printing despatch notes and invoices, and can be relatively cheap to buy and operate.

3. Install a loudspeaker link between telephone enquiry point and warehouse. Have the storeman look to see if stock is available, then reserve it for that order number.

PLANNING

Simulation is a way of exploring the merits of alternative courses of action before committing yourself. Simulation may be used to answer questions such as:

How many loading bays should I install in my new warehouse? Too few bays may lead to excessive delays for vehicles waiting to load; too many bays means money and space wasted.

In which sequence should I programme production batches in a machine shop to make best use of the available machine groups?

What would be the effect on inventory and customer service if I introduce a particular system of inventory control?

What will be the effect on liquidity and profit if the company grows at 5 per cent per annum over the next five years?

To start with you will probably need the help of a competent analyst, statistician, OR man or accountant to help you.

You should then set out to solve the problem using pencil and paper until you both really understand what you want to do. Then if the computation is going to be very great (over five man weeks' work, say, or is likely to be required frequently), you should consider using a computer. This is how you might tackle the four simulations set out above:

1. *How many loading bays?*

The two major variable factors in estimating the number of loading bays required are:

the interval between successive vehicle arrivals
the time taken to load the vehicles

Say thirty vehicles arrive per day. If they arrived exactly evenly spaced, we could calculate the number of bays required as soon as we knew the loading time, but in practice we must cope with the peaks when several vehicles arrive within a short time.

Use random number tables to generate the interval between

vehicles arriving. See what would happen if you had only two bays, by noting the time each successive vehicle arrives, putting it into a free bay or noting the delay if it has to wait.

ARRIVALS			ALLOCATION TO SERVICE				
				BAY 1		BAY 2	
Random No. (from list)	Arrival Intvl (from table)	Time of Arrival (min)	DELAY TO LORRY	Start Loading	End Loading	Start Loading	End Loading
3	16	16		16	46		
8	19	35				35	65
0	14	49		49	79		
0	14	63	2			65	95
1	15	78	1	79	109		
4	17	95				95	125
4	17	112		112	142		
1	15	127				127	157
9	20	147		147	177		
0						161	191

FIG. 16 Simulation of Lorry Arrivals – Manual System

Extract from List of Random Numbers

38 00	14 41	90 60	25 71	32 43	83 81	30 51	43 63	89 08	98 66
31 70	42 92	74 21	27 31	57 40	60 75	96 16	86 82	80 32	00 00
06 99	75 04	74 31	15 57	80 78	79 27	34 25	63 87	35 08	89 28
62 36	87 84	42 86	48 99	72 28	95 25	84 30	50 32	33 78	77 64
82 29	39 21	91 35	01 74	20 41	84 47	70 04	45 72	22 03	72 80

Table for Converting Random Numbers to Arrival Intervals

Random Number	*Arrival Interval*
0	14
1	15
2 or 3	16
4 or 5	17
6 or 7	18
8	19
9	20

The arrival of vehicles and operation of two loading bays is illustrated in this example. Random numbers (from the list shown) are converted into arrival intervals using the simplified table above. In the simulation it is assumed that every vehicle takes 30 minutes to load. It will be seen that two vehicles were delayed (for two minutes and one minute respectively) because the bays had not quite completed loading the previous vehicles.

THIS PROGRAM SIMULATES THE ARRIVAL OF LORRIES AT TWO WAREHOUSES. AT BOTH WAREHOUSES THE AVERAGE INTERVAL BETWEEN ARRIVALS IS 17 MINUTES. AT THE FIRST THE INTERVAL RANGES FROM 78 MINUTES BETWEEN ARRIVALS DOWN TO Ø. AT THE SECOND.THE RANGE IS 27 MINUTES DOWN TO 9.

THE PROGRAM SIMULATES THE DELAYS THAT WOULD BE EXPERIENCED AT EITHER WAREHOUSE DURING A WEEKS OPERATION USING DIFFERENT NUMBERS OF LOADING BAYS.

```
WHICH WAREHOUSE WOULD YOU LIKE TO TRY? 2
HOW MANY LOADING BAYS? 2


   WHSE 2  BAYS 2   IDLE   951

   NO.    NO.OVER  TOTAL   ANNUAL
LORRIES 20 MINS   DELAY    COST
   139        Ø       47      58



WHICH WAREHOUSE WOULD YOU LIKE TO TRY? 2
HOW MANY LOADING BAYS? 2


   WHSE 2  BAYS 2   IDLE   77Ø

   NO.    NO.OVER  TOTAL   ANNUAL
LORRIES 2Ø MINS   DELAY    COST
   146        Ø       71      88
```

```
WHICH WAREHOUSE WOULD YOU LIKE TO TRY? 1
HOW MANY LOADING BAYS? 2

  WHSE 1  BAYS 2    IDLE    524

  NO.     NO.OVER   TOTAL    ANNUAL
LORRIES 2Ø MINS   DELAY     COST
   169       98      5569     6961



WHICH WAREHOUSE WOULD YOU LIKE TO TRY? 1
HOW MANY LOADING BAYS? 3

  WHSE 1  BAYS 3    IDLE   2187

  NO.     NO.OVER   TOTAL    ANNUAL
LORRIES 2Ø MINS   DELAY     COST
   174       11       936     117Ø



WHICH WAREHOUSE WOULD YOU LIKE TO TRY? 1
HOW MANY LOADING BAYS? 4

  WHSE 1  BAYS 4    IDLE   5853

  NO.     NO.OVER   TOTAL    ANNUAL
LORRIES 2Ø MINS   DELAY     COST
   141        1       1Ø9      136
```

FIG. 17 Simulation of Lorry Arrivals – Computer Model

At the end of the day calculate the total time lorries spend waiting and also the number of lorries that have to wait an excessive time – say over twenty minutes. Repeat these steps with three bays, then four bays each for say twenty days' operation until a pattern emerges. Decide how many bays are required by balancing the cost of delays against the cost of building and manning an extra bay.

In this example the job could be done manually with a few weeks' effort so the computer would not be justified. But add some more variables such as different loading times or waiting to get to the warehouse via a level crossing, and it soon becomes impractical to do it by hand.

2. *Programming production batches*

The sequence in which jobs are presented in a machine shop may make all the difference to the overall machine utilisation. The aim of a simulation is to try out alternative sequences before committing yourself to the production programme. The outline steps are:

Divide the machines into groups and calculate an average throughput per group.

Draw a network for all jobs to be done (and those in progress) showing the logical sequence of flow between machine groups and how much capacity is required of each group.

Draw a bar chart showing the projected load on the machines of existing work.

Take a new job and schedule it on to the chart, taking account of delays in getting jobs from one machine group to another, the amount of work in progress that can be allowed to accumulate between operations, and the logical sequence of operations dictated by the network.

Repeat this scheduling with each succeeding job.

This operation will reveal the major bottlenecks and will give ideas on how the loading can be improved. Ideally you should now try a second schedule which improves on the first, then a third and a fourth.

In practice, this manual scheduling can become very time-consuming and it may be appropriate to carry out the simulation on a computer if a large number of jobs and machines are involved. This means writing a program which will carry out the same scheduling operation on the computer as the manual one described above. The difference is that the computer can go through many more combinations of jobs in a short time to arrive at a good solution.

This sort of computer operation is usually best done using a time-sharing bureau, because the best result is obtained when the manager and the computer 'interact'. You tell the computer to try out, say, five different job sequences; it works out the resultant loadings and highlights both spare capacity and any bottleneck jobs. Using your knowledge of the different jobs you then try another sequence to see if there is any improvement. And so on until an acceptable overall efficiency is achieved.

You may be surprised that the computer cannot do it all. In some cases it can, but more commonly it is too difficult to specify all the rules – special operator skills for example. So the manager needs to superimpose his own knowledge and judgement on the arithmetic ability of the computer.

3. *Inventory simulation*

Before committing your company to a new and possibly expensive inventory control system, it is desirable to estimate the expected benefits. Would a less sophisticated system provide most of the benefits at greatly reduced cost? It would be impractical to simulate the proposed systems on every one of the stock items. A random sample of, say, 1–5 per cent of the items will usually be sufficient to give an accurate picture of the whole. The outline procedure for the simulation is:

> Gather information about the sample items over the last twelve months – customer orders, stockouts, average stock levels, obsolescence, stock losses.
>
> Specify a number of different stock control methods. They will usually consist of three parts:
>
> forecasting demand
> deciding when to re-order
> deciding how much to re-order

Forecasting demand can be done in different ways (for example, exponential smoothing or even the manager's opinion), as can deciding the degree of control and the level of customer service desired.

Starting from twelve months back, see what would have happened if one or all of the proposed systems had been used, measure the number of stockouts (customer service), the average stock level (capital investment) and the cost of control (running costs).

Compare the results of the different methods for different stock categories (expensive, cheap, large, small, high volume, low volume).

Estimate also the costs of running the different methods and compare them with existing costs.

MOTOR COMPONENTS - CONTRIBUTION ANALYSIS

TYPE 1 IF YOU WISH TO SEE TOTALS ONLY
2 TO SKIP FIRST ALLOCATION, OTHERWISE 0?0

	SPARE-MFD	SPARES-BO	ACCES-MFD	ACCESS-BO	TOTALS
SALES UNITS	2100	900	150	240	3390
ORDER LINES	1400	.600	100	160	2260
STOCK VALUE	1170	630	180	220	2200
SALES REV	3775	1625	225	375	6000
---------	-------	-------	-------	-------	-------
VARIABLE COSTS					
-SALES/ADMIN	173	74	12	20	
-STOCKINVEST	70	38	11	13	
-PRODN/BO	2548	1250	152	250	
-DEBTORS	70	30	4	7	
TOTAL COSTS	2862	1392	179	290	
---------	-------	-------	-------	-------	-------
CONTRIBUTION	913	233	46	85	1277
CON.PER UNIT	0.43	0.26	0.31	0.35	0.38
LIQUIDITY	0	0	0	0	0

TOTAL CONTRIBUTION	1277.00
FIXED COSTS	1220.00
NET PROFIT	57.00
PROFIT/SALES %	0.95
IMPROVED LIQUIDITY	0.00

FIG. 18 Company Financial Model

The first part of this model (above) shows the company's contribution to profit (1277) analysed into the contributions from the four main product groups. Figure 15 showed the effect of adjusting the sales and other figures.

Even if a computer will not be used in the final inventory control system, it may be appropriate to use one for the simulation. Most of the major computer manufacturers and computer bureaux have standard inventory control 'packages'. These packages allow you to carry out the simulation without the need to write your own programs from scratch.

4. *Company financial model*
A principal feature of corporate planning is the development of alternative company strategies. Managers still have the task of selecting the most appropriate strategy, and simulation helps them see the likely effects of alternative courses of action before making a decision. Here is one way it might be done:

Split the company or division into major product groups.

Identify fixed and variable costs and establish some basis for splitting the variable costs between the product groups.

Calculate the contribution to profit from each product group.

Try out different growth and profitability patterns for each product group and check the investment required to finance this growth.

Make sure the final solution makes business sense, e.g. it is very easy to test on the computer the effect of doubling sales but doubling sales in the market place is a very different matter.

This type of simulation is known as a company model. While it is quite possible to do the simulation manually, carrying it out on a computer has a number of advantages. In a large company with many divisions the calculations may be difficult and even in a smaller company a computer enables breaking down into smaller units. It is also possible to consider a large number of alternatives but, perhaps more importantly, it is possible to test extremes: for example, what would be the effect if a whole division were closed?

Constructing a computer model of this type may cost £3000–£5000 or more, but in comparison with the amount of investment at stake this can be money well spent. But a word of warning. Experience

Packages allow you to carry out the simulation without the need to write your own programs from scratch

has shown that **the simpler the model the greater the benefit.** A complex model can be as difficult to understand as the real-life situation, which defeats the object.

In conclusion, simulation is a 'problem-solving' tool and computers are well suited to removing the clerical drudgery from the operation.

Each example illustrates that the right way to use the computer is to take the problem one stage at a time. First work out what you are trying to achieve with pencil and paper. Then get the computer people to help you when the calculations begin to get too arduous.

SUMMARY

The purpose of this chapter has been not only to show how the computer is often applied but also to show how such common jobs are approached. Data processing using computers is accepted business practice for such applications as stock control, bank accounting, insurance policy administration, etc. – the mechanisation of reorganised clerical work. Management information is still a controversial and complex area which is often misunderstood or misinterpreted. Its purpose is practical day-to-day control of an organisation's activities but the higher the level of decision, and also the longer the time covered, the less likely is a computer to be helpful. There are several uses for on-line computer power which give a user immediate access, and this is becoming increasingly popular, not just for management information work. On-line power is available via terminals to a large central processor or from mini computers, which in turn may act as satellites or 'hyper-intelligent terminals' to a large machine.

As a general rule, it is sensible always to start computerisation with the mechanical drudgery of data processing (in a sales context it would perhaps be invoicing), then to move to using the information by-product of this for management control (in this example, sales analysis), and finally to elaborate the process to problem solving and planning (e.g. marketing models).

Cheap timesharing bureaux with sophisticated packages and experienced managers can make it possible for a company to leap straight into problem solving. But in practice the company must be able to absorb the information that the changes may entail, which often may require the existence of some methodical data processing and the availability of control information to measure subsequent performance.

Chapter 4

What Sort of Computer For Me?

The manager confronted with the problem of getting his work on to a computer is presented with a bewildering choice – a large machine or a small; centralised or decentralised computer power; his own machine or a service bureau? The range of options is bewildering even for an experienced man, but you can minimise the risk of getting it wrong.

The problem is where to start. Beware of asking a salesman; he is more likely to sell you what he has than what is necessarily good for you.

If you were buying a new car and had never driven one before, or even been in one, prudence suggests that first of all the one to learn on may not be the one you would eventually want to own. For example, if you were to learn on a Jaguar you might collect some very expensive dents. Secondly, until you have experience of driving the car you may not know which one suits your needs. For example, if you are shifting loads, a pick-up would be more use to you than a GT, even if the GT does look more attractive. All in all you would probably prefer to learn to drive on someone else's car and then hire various models to make sure that what you are going to buy is what you really want.

There is a fair analogy here with learning to use a computer. You need to learn the disciplines, keeping your options open for the future, and one way of doing it is to use a service bureau.

USING A SERVICE BUREAU

Service bureaux exist to sell computer time to companies, some of which own their own computer as well. In addition they usually provide a range of programming, systems and consultancy services. Typically you pay by the hour and get quantity discounts for long contracts. The rates vary from £20 an hour to £100 and more, depending on the size of the computer. At first sight these rates may seem expensive, but as with a taxi you can take a lot of journeys before you equal the cost of owning a car.

The first-time computer user should avoid learning on his own computer.

Only if the cost builds up should you get your own machine. There may of course be problems with a service bureau but these are likely to be fewer than using your own machine, at least initially. It is the business of a service bureau to be professional and you have yet to learn.

Installing and running a computer efficiently is a very demanding job, equivalent in many ways to planning and controlling production in a small engineering company. Equally, developing systems expertise is demanding and difficult. So it is again sensible not to try both difficult tasks together.

WHERE TO START

Start with a useful but not too difficult job where the responsibilities are not shared by different factions in the business. Start possibly with sales statistics with the marketing manager responsible, or the sales, purchase and nominal ledgers with the accountant responsible. You should probably not start with stock control, an inherently difficult area, or production control which is a very difficult area. Payroll will not teach you much that is useful for your other applications, and personnel records become unnecessarily complex on a computer.

WHAT CAN YOU EXPECT TO LEARN?

Using a bureau you can expect to learn:

- the rules for devising coding structures and how to apply codes to products and to customers
- the disciplines of accuracy and the turnround of errors and corrections
- the hidden costs of computing

The hidden costs tend to be concerned with what happens when you make mistakes. Errors in specifying requirements correctly may mean costly reprogramming at a later stage. Errors in input data may mean re-running the job to get it absolutely right – again at extra cost. An extraordinary amount of management time will also be spent in both specifying requirements and sorting out problems.

SECURITY AND CONFIDENTIALITY

Service bureaux would go out of business if they were to get a reputation for disclosing clients' secrets but it is difficult to make sure that mistakes are never made – the sort of thing that can happen is that one of your reports gets put in the pile for somebody else by mistake. Check the bureau's procedures to ensure quality control and to minimise the risk of error. Have a chat with other customers to find out what their experience is and make sure that the bureau pays every attention to the disciplines to ensure confidentiality.

A professional bureau will automatically arrange to have security copies of all the magnetic tapes and discs held at a different location. You should go through with them what happens in the event of fire or other disaster and how you will be placed. They should be able to answer the questions comfortably to your satisfaction.

USING PACKAGES

Service bureaux often help first-time computer users by offering packaged programs for areas such as payroll and sales accounting. And packages are of course not exclusive to service bureaux; you can buy them from a variety of sources for running on your own computer. Why then does anyone program their own application at all instead of using a package? Why not have just one manufacturing package? Instinctively one feels that for each computer user to write his own routines individually must be an enormous national waste of effort.

And yet few packages have been successful. Those that have, tend to be in highly structured areas such as linear programming, statistical analysis and payroll where the rules are explicit, and in certain computer aids like programming languages. Packages are less widely used in areas of discretion.

It may be easier to see the difficulty in using a package in real life if we again use a transport analogy. Suppose you want to go from London to Birmingham. Clearly there is no need to learn to drive or to blaze a trail, as the simplest way is to take the train. But if you live in High Wycombe, 31 miles from London, it may be easier to take a car after all because although the train goes fast from London to Birmingham you are not starting at London and may not want to finish at the centre of Birmingham.

So it is with packages. To write a package that goes 90 per cent of the way is fairly easy. To satisfy every user's needs means adding (impossibly) complex access routines at either end. If you do need to go to Birmingham regularly and want to take the comfortable train you can move house (change your business ways) or you might settle for driving after all (give up the package and program the job yourself).

Again, the destination of a journey is not always clear. You might take a holiday bus with the destination 'France', hoping, aided by the salesman no doubt, to get some good way to the Mediterranean. Imagine your disappointment if the bus stops at Paris or even Calais. It all depends on what you, the travel agent and the bus operator understand by 'France'. With some of the more advanced packages it is easy enough to know the general direction they are going; it is much less easy to find out until you are well into them exactly how far they are going to go to meet your business needs.

Here then are some of the questions to ask when buying a package:

1. What is the job I want done and where do I have particular needs?

2. What precisely is the job the package does?

3. Are the differences small enough for us to continue looking at it?

4. If I adopt it, what changes are required in the way I run my business?

5. Can the package be adapted at reasonable cost?

6. How much is it going to cost to develop, install and use?

7. How reliable is it going to be, who else is using it, what is the reputation of the vendor?

The way to set about answering these questions is to select the most likely packages to do the job you want and then to carry out a system of exhaustive tests which go into progressively more detail. Even if you decide against it the work is not wasted; you will have learned a tremendous amount for developing your own system.

In most cases you will find that the relatively different costs of buying a package or writing your own programs are swamped by the major costs of introducing change – whichever way it is done.

CHOICE OF HARDWARE

When looking at the different types of machines available it is convenient to divide them into three main groups:

1. Accounting machines and their derivatives
2. Small business and mini computers
3. Main frame computers

This grouping is necessarily a bit arbitrary and there are many computers which are on the borderline between the different groups. But though the divisions may blur at the edges the groups provide a basis for assessing alternatives.

ACCOUNTING MACHINES AND THEIR DERIVATIVES

The computers developed from accounting machines tend to have a keyboard, ledger card posting and the ability to do quite complex calculations. Frequently the ledger card contains magnetic stripes on the back so that prices, balances and even descriptions can be 'memorised' on the card and do not need to be typed every time by the girl. The advantage of these machines is that there is a visible and accessible record of the transactions on the ledger card, so queries can be answered easily. Moreover, it is clearly under the control of the relevant office manager.

These machines tend to be good for 'one file' applications, such as payroll, hire purchase accounting, building society mortgages, banking. They tend to be clumsy when two files are needed, for example, a customer file and a stock file to be referenced at the same time in a stock control application. The machines cannot sort postings but summary analyses are possible.

These computers are sometimes called visible record computers (VRCs) and there is a well-known law (well known to the authors anyway) which says that if you have ordered one you need two and if you have ordered two you need four. This is because their rate of posting all the ancillary jobs means that they process at about half the speed the salesman promises. But since some VRCs have facilities like line printers, discs, tape, etc., the distinction between them and small business computers gets blurred.

SMALL BUSINESS AND MINI COMPUTERS

Small business computers feature a keyboard, input by means of cards or paper tape, quite powerful calculations and quite substantial disc storage.

Prices start below £30,000 and can go up to about £100,000. You get a fair amount of business support from suppliers for genuine small computers which can do a whole variety of jobs. They tend to be programmed in languages known as COBOL or RPG, and if they are not the manufacturer often does the programming for you. They are quite a practical way in for the smaller company but they do need to be run like a production shop – they cannot be run informally very easily. One man must be clearly responsible for them.

There are also some mini computers which started off with scientific origins and so you tend to get a lot of computer for the money but relatively little business support. For the company already experienced in computers they are very suitable. As they were designed for process control, twenty-four hours a day, they tend to be very reliable and are good for on-line jobs with terminals. Mini computers are not really for mini companies. They work best doing one job at a time or doing one job in a rather larger company that can justify having it dedicated to one job. They can also sometimes be used as hyper-intelligent terminals to the company's main computer. However, it should be remembered that there are a large number of suppliers of VRCs and minis (over 50 at the last count) and they vary enormously in size and quality. Anyone thinking of buying equipment of this kind should take particular care. Perhaps the best simple test to apply is to visit a number of the supplier's other customers who have already used for some months the equipment proposed for you and ask some searching questions (you may even discover that *you* are the equipment's first customer; in this case avoid it like the plague).

MAIN FRAME COMPUTERS

Main frame computers are from £80,000 upwards. They all have large computer memory and a substantial number of tapes and discs. It is normally possible to run several programs concurrently. They are capable of doing almost any type of job, process large quantities of data comfortably and can have the other two types of computer connected to them to allow local access to centralised power if that is required. However if you are considering an on-line application it is worth checking the cost of a mini computer against the cost of extending your main frame.

CENTRALISATION OR DECENTRALISATION

Computers can be organised these days in almost any way that you wish. You can have centralised computers or decentralised computers. You can have large computers or small computers. You can buy a computer for just one application. So the way you organise it is less constrained by physical rather than business needs. You can go further, and separate logical centralisation or decentralisation from the physical centralisation or decentralisation.

Where the machines are physically sited tends to be a matter of cost. Where the machines are controlled ought to be in tune with the business philosophy. **As a general rule, if there is decentralised decision-making the computers should be logically decentralised.**

But do not fall into the trap of thinking that a business with branches is necessarily decentralised. For example, clearing banks with centralised clearing and centralised control over borrowing and lending limits are good candidates for centralised computing power. Some building societies have a tradition of centralisation and so a central computer for them is appropriate. Other building societies have a tradition of local decision-making and when they have installed centralised computers there have been reports of problems in adjusting to a changed management style. Similarly a company working in one location may be conducting four or five discrete types of business which are logically separate. In such a case they ought to have their computing separate even if they physically use one computer. The chart below shows how it is possible for, say, a company with four divisions to be logically or physically centralised or decentralised.

	LOGICALLY DECENTRALISED	LOGICALLY CENTRALISED
PHYSICALLY DECENTRALISED	4 small business computers each with different programs	4 identical local computers with common programs, perhaps a central small computer for summary purposes
PHYSICALLY CENTRALISED	4 terminals to a main frame computer at the centre each running different programs. Or central main frame computer with 4 different sets of programs	Central main frame computer with common programs for the four divisions

HAVING AN IN-HOUSE COMPUTER

To use even a modest accounting machine successfully requires considerable discipline in the accounts office. If the work is not streamed and does not flow evenly then there is wasted time and inefficient working at the machine. So it is with computers, however small. Studies have shown that they cannot be used informally with any success. If you are going to have an in-house computer it is going to be quite an expensive business and there is only one way to do it, that is, right first time.

The costs being what they are – see Chapter 2 on value for money – you cannot afford to get it wrong; it is far too expensive in direct terms, to say nothing of the cost of the consequent chaos.

CHOOSING THE MANUFACTURER

When selecting equipment and a manufacturer there is one golden rule to observe – never to blaze a trail. Let somebody else be the first to try out a new machine or a new package and get it working. Many people believe that they must be up with the times and that to have an old machine would be a significant disadvantage compared with a competitor who has just installed the latest model. However, the

Never blaze a trail. Let somebody else be the first to try out a new machine or a new package

objective is to have satisfactory systems which do not disrupt the company and which solve the business problems. The history of computers suggests that a new generation of machines advances business problem solving very little. After all the machine is not an end in itself but a means to an end, so what you want is something really reliable. In that way you will be ahead of your competitors.

We can assume that computer suppliers desire what we desire – satisfactory equipment working smoothly for satisfied customers. But it is only prudent to plan on the basis that things will go wrong. Experience shows the following points are most likely to cause trouble:

* Either the machine or the air conditioning will be late.

* It will take the machine or the air conditioning at least two months to settle in satisfactorily.

* You and the manufacturer will disagree over machine performance. So establish your idea of reasonable down time before you get the equipment – not after.

* Inexperienced engineers will be sent to solve your problems so establish who the engineer is to call when he has not fixed the problem within, say, four hours. Engineers like working where they have a small office, a telephone and access to a tea machine, so why not supply these and steal a march on the other places that might lure him away. (This is known as the 'nesting box' principle.)

* Assume that the machinery will be inexpertly installed so that, for example, they might inadvertently put the printer between the air conditioning coming in and the tape drives – so all the fluff and dust from the printer gets blown directly at the tape drives – leading to inevitable reading errors.

* A manufacturers' best staff are either salesmen or have left to join customers, so the systems and programming support you get will tend to be from trainees. In any case, assume manufacturers know very little about your business and beware of their offers of putting the first application on – it will probably all need re-doing within twelve months.

* Every time a major new application is added to the computer you are going to get machine trouble. Do not ask why, it just happens that way.

* You will need a machine for program testing so make sure it is installed and available before you place your order – otherwise you run the risk of tedious long-range testing or of waiting for your own machine.

* Avoid demonstrations and mock-ups. You will learn little from them which is of any value. Go and see the thing *working* with

other users. That is the only way you will find out whether it is really working or if you have been sold a line.

* Beware of making important buying decisions on the basis of attractive looking promises.

Do not believe that if you follow this advice perhaps it is all going to be very dull and easy.

SUMMARY – HOW TO AVOID SOME OF THE TRAPS

1. Avoid anything new. Never be in the first wave.

2. All jobs are going to take twice as long on the machine as the salesman thinks; this is particularly true of visible record computers where the time is usually much more critical.

3. Get experience before you get committed to a machine; preferably always start with a service bureau.

4. Mini companies do not have mini problems. They have all the problems of a larger company on a smaller scale so do not be fooled into thinking that mini computers will solve all the problems of a mini company, or vice versa.

5. Avoid demonstrations and mock-ups. You are not going to learn much which is of any use to you. Talk to customers who can show it to you working.

Part II

How to Get it All on to a Computer

A computer is a versatile general purpose machine that must be told what to do in each individual case. So before it can become useful a computer system must be tailored to a particular application and programmed to the user's needs.

Before this can be done, the job itself and the company's methods must be systematised and organised to suit the pedantic logic of the computer. In the process both the methods of carrying out the tasks and the organisation itself will inevitably change, but any disruption this causes is compensated for by the increased rationality of going about the work and by the bringing into the open tacit rules (and the way they get bent and ignored), long-established confusions and unresolved internal contradictions.

This process of organisation is carried out by the managers and systems analysts who, having made the existing system more efficient, must again re-examine the problems to see whether the computer is still necessary.

If it is, the whole process of acquisition, installation and use must be managed at least as carefully and rigorously as any other substantial investment. This is because the computer not only represents heavy spending but also carries within it the possibilities of wreaking havoc with an organisation if mismanaged, or of providing considerable benefits if properly and intelligently used.

So the steps in installing or using a computer are: set up proper project management, invest in careful analysis of the company and the aspect to be computerised, draw up the method of work to go on to the machine, and then program the task. None of these – the project-orientated first part, to the production-orientated end use – can be handed over entirely to the computer experts. That would be a sure recipe for later trouble; the user manager must be involved from start to finish.

Chapter 5

Systems Design and Control

PROJECT MANAGEMENT

The first step in installing a computer is to set up effective project control mechanisms. The analysis of the company's systems, programming and computer installation is a major investment within which several detailed projects need managing.

In following our suggestions always bear in mind that the purpose of all these processes is to reduce the risk of unpleasant surprises at later stages – safety belts can save on doctors' bills. So these outline recommendations may need adaptation to a particular case, or may require supplementing with further control mechanisms.

Effective control has five principal ingredients:

Clearly defined project aims

Division of the job into stages that can be supervised (too large a piece is hard to keep track of and difficult to adapt to changing circumstances)

Subdivision into still smaller chunks of a week or two to monitor progress

Separation of routine parts of the installation from research elements

Clear documentation to ensure the work is keeping to schedule and course

But mechanisms are operated by people and even the most ingenious schemes can be – and have been – wrecked by inexpert or unco-operative staff. So the second aspect of project management is the setting up of a team to be responsible for the systems analysis and computer installation.

Once the people and mechanisms are agreed, the detailed examination of the organisation's procedures and aims can start and alternative solutions assessed. Preliminary investigations (see Chapter 2) may have indicated the computer as feasible but a closer look at each process may suggest a simpler or cheaper solution. Systems analysis requires a flexible approach and an open mind.

1. EFFECTIVE CONTROL

All development work must be carried out as a project. This means clear objectives, an agreed start date, nominated resources, a fixed completion date and a post-implementation review.

Three further points:

First, the right size of project is not much larger than your last successful project.

Second, few projects should be allowed to take longer than one year. If it is over two years, then break it into two or more sub-projects. Experience shows that projects taking over two years have a distinctly lower chance of successful completion, and the odds lengthen with time.

Third, while it can be a good idea to establish applications groups (a group to concentrate on one application area), beware of creating an 'application continuum' in which projects never stop.

2. PROJECTS BROKEN DOWN INTO STAGES

All projects must be further broken down into stages:

as an aid to estimating time and resources

as a means of monitoring progress

and so as a way of planning to anticipate late running

Each stage must be a clearly defined break point requiring written evidence of progress.

In developing computer systems the stages are typically:

Survey stage, which is concerned with problem identification. The end product is the Survey Report.

Evaluation stage, which is concerned with developing alternative solutions. The end product is a Functional Description which shows how the selected solution will work in both a technical and a business sense.

Specification stage, which is concerned with writing very detailed business specifications for every procedure.

Programming stage, which includes programming strategy, programming and basic testing.

Implementation stage, which includes full system logic testing, volume and date testing, parallel running, file conversion, user training and final cut-over.

3. SHORT INTERVAL SCHEDULING

Short interval scheduling (breaking down jobs into small components) is one of the keys to project management.

A case history will illustrate how effective it can be – this example was in a data preparation department where they were punching input data into paper tape.

There were fourteen girls in the department, which was heavily overloaded, with a continuous backlog of work. A new supervisor introduced short interval scheduling. She would hand out the work in the following way:

'Here are 100 orders for you to punch. It will take about half a minute per order, so you should have them done in 50 minutes. The time is now 9 o'clock; I would like you back with the job done by 10 o'clock.'

The girl could see she had been given a fair job with a fair time, and with the responsibility to achieve a target, she almost invariably did it on time and within agreed quality (errors) standards.

The supervisor, however, continuously monitored her own estimates. She would weigh the punched paper tape to establish its length and thus how many key strokes had actually gone into the job.

The effectiveness of this approach can be judged by the results. Three months after the supervisor was appointed, the number of punch girls had been reduced from fourteen to seven. Instead of a backlog of work, the girls seemed to have time on their hands and they did the work efficiently.

Notice that the supervisor used the minimum of forms and controls. She had figured out the work content of each job and used this to set realistic targets which she expected the girls to achieve.

The same sort of techniques should apply to project management. The work should be so broken down that the project manager virtually never hands out more than two weeks' work. The only exception can be during the early survey stages and even then a programme of visits should be established by the systems analyst in advance.

The whole object is to get the project team used to hitting target dates – not missing them.

4. IDENTIFY INNOVATION IN PROJECTS

While many projects are concerned with well-understood hardware and software, some projects contain a high 'research' element. This may be because you are planning to use some new software program or because you plan to use (say) an on-line enquiry system for the first time.

It is difficult enough to get computer projects working successfully using well-known techniques. You should therefore identify the innovation element in projects, separate it from the well understood, and set about minimising the uncertainty. Talk to other users in detail, or experiment with your own systems – but either way, mount a 'research project' to understand the new technology before setting up the real project to implement an advanced new application.

PROJECT NAME:

PURPOSE OF PROJECT:

PERSON INITIATING PROJECT:

PROJECT STAGE:

TERMS OF REFERENCE:

PROJECT MANAGER AND TEAM:

SUPERVISING MANAGER:

USER EXECUTIVE:

START DATE:

COMPLETION DATE:

COSTS:

	HARD BUDGET THIS STAGE			SOFT BUDGET REST OF PROJECT		
	Days/ hours	Rate	£	Days/ hours	Rate	£
Internal Manpower						
External Manpower						
Computer Time						
Capital Expenditure						

AUTHORISED:

DATE:

FIG. 19 Project Authorisation

Hill Samuel & Co Limited

Activity Time Estimate

Project Name:					Date:
					Project Code
Activity:			Responsible		Activity Code
Task/Milestone	Budget days	Spent to date	Actual days	Finish date	Comment
Review by:					
TOTAL					

Prepared by .... Approved by ....

HS/10783/MNS/3 74

FIG. 20 Activity Time Estimate

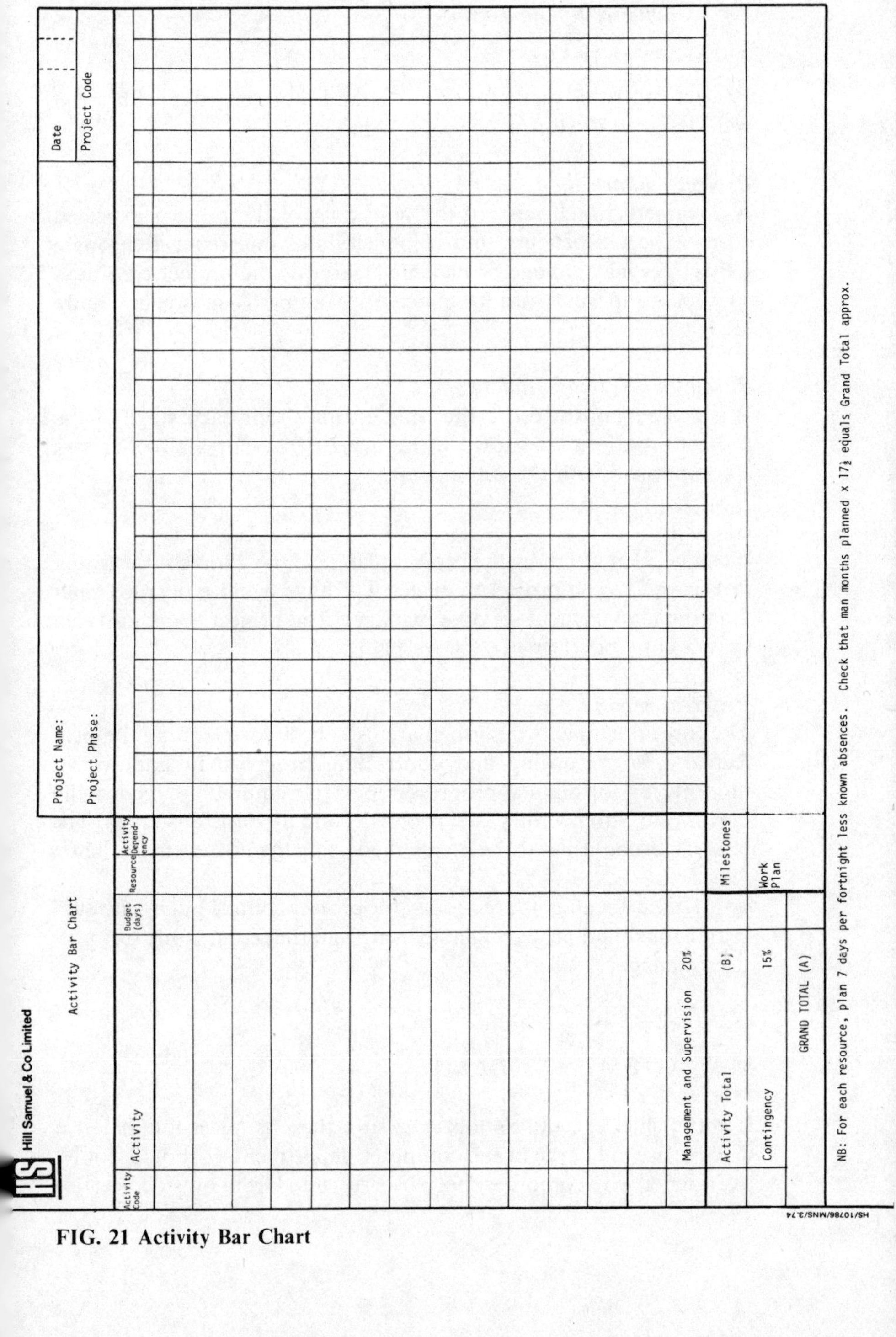

FIG. 21 Activity Bar Chart

5. DOCUMENTATION

Project control is made much easier and more effective with a few well-designed documents:

Project authorisation
A document which sets out the objectives of the project, expected costs, expected benefits, and responsibilities for seeing it through. Objectives may change or become clearer as the project continues so allocate space to restate them. An example is shown in Figure 19.

Resource and time estimates
It is convenient to record the time estimates for each stage of the project on a form as shown in Figure 20. This form also requires a comparison with the actual time.

Bar chart
It can be useful to show the project plan as a bar chart as illustrated in Figure 21. The project manager will have a more detailed plan than the management services manager. The project team may also have a copy of all or part of the plan.

Progress reports
The three documents described are used both for planning the project and for recording and controlling progress. In addition, a monthly or fortnightly progress report is required to record the current situation, anticipated problems and all decisions taken. The report can conveniently be marshalled using the document in Figure 22.

All these documents are needed for project control but are no substitute for sound project management, and that comes only from the user manager.

MANAGEMENT TEAM

It is the chief executive's job to ensure there is a sensible balance of expertise in charge of the computer department. It should not be overloaded with computer specialists recruited from outside because

Hill Samuel & Co Limited

Project Progress Report

	Date
Project Title:	Project Code

Current Situation:

Early Warning of Problem Areas:

Summary of all agreements / commitments made since last report:

Resources used this Month					
Days	Resource Type	Rate	Charge	Old Estimated Completion Date	
				Latest Estimate of Completion Date	
				Budget days this Phase	(A)
				Cross total Estimated Effort	(B)
				Contingency remaining	(A-B)
				Tick documents attached:	
				Activity Bar Chart	☐
				Activity Progress Records	☐
	Totals this month			Reasons for Date/Cost Changes	☐
	Spent to last month			Minutes of all Meetings	☐
	Spent to date			Copies of significant correspondence	☐

Resources required/released next two months:	Project Leader (sig) ....
	Supervisor ....
	Manager, Projects ....

HS/10784/MNS/3.74

FIG. 22 Project Progress Report

computer people are sometimes not good at project management, partly because the computer profession has been slow to see the need for sound management. In addition the outsiders will have little knowledge of the organisation and may indeed have little business experience.

On the other hand the people already in the company will take time to gain technical experience. So a balance must be struck to enable each side to educate the other and bring its skills to bear. For failure to plan a new system properly and to manage its introduction can jeopardise its success and will almost certainly cost a great deal in extra resources to rescue it at the last moment.

Until the computer people's ideas and recommendations are as commonplace and as well understood as those of, say, an organisation and methods man, and as open to intelligent and informed judgements and criticisms, some bridge between management and computer disciplines needs to be built.

The choice of data processing manager is therefore critical. He has to have extensive technical ability as well as considerable management expertise and skills, so the first-time user is unlikely to find him within the company. There are two sensible options: find an existing senior manager who is genuinely committed to the computer installation and put him in charge, with a first-rate technical man recruited to be his second-in-command; or find a hot-shot computer specialist with managerial experience (some management ability is indispensable) and put one of your existing managers as his number two. Either way, ensure that the senior computer men and their department are plugged into the management structure.

All too often, what happens is that the computer staff design a system in splendid isolation and are forced into a sales exercise in 'securing management acceptance'. Systems analysts will not understand all the facts, all the rules, all the problems, so the system may be an entirely academic construction, unrelated to the needs of the business. At best it will have a number of errors and omissions in it.

Unless the departmental managers who are to use the system have contributed to its design, they will not be committed to making it work and may even let it fail, just to show how well they did the job before the computer.

Managers' involvement is essential at the survey stage. They can help the analyst to understand the existing system and should themselves use the opportunity critically to examine the validity of each task. They will also be committed to making it work which is very important. Managers will also be guided to decide what additional information they require from the new systems.

The manager of the department where work is to be transferred to a computer must take an active part in the work. His first job is to clear the way for the investigating team. All staff should be briefed on the project and asked to co-operate. If there are to be redundancies, the company's policy should be made clear to all likely to be affected; if there is no question of redundancy, the staff should be reassured on this point.

A typical example of how project planning can fail through the uninvolvement of user departments occurred in a company we know. The computer department had put up a sketchy proposal for stock control by computer. The cost of the exercise, it was stated, would be recouped partly by staff savings and partly by reducing the stock levels.

When we arrived on the scene the project had been running on the computer for some months and was causing a great deal of concern. The stores manager complained that the computer reports on stock levels were so inaccurate that he had to retain staff to keep handwritten records. The data processing manager retorted that receipts and issues of stock were not being accurately recorded 'so it's no wonder that the computer produces wrong results'. The stores manager replied that it was impossible to make accurate records partly because the forms were badly designed and partly because his staff did not have enough time.

Neither side was prepared to accept responsibility for the failure. The stores manager's attitude was, 'They put up this proposal and promised us a wonderful system; we accepted it in good faith. But in practice, it just doesn't work.' The data processing manager said, 'It's a perfectly good system; it just isn't being used right.'

THE STEERING COMMITTEE

One very simple and effective aid in getting the data processing department's activities integrated with the rest of the business is the computer steering committee. It should meet ideally about once a month and should comprise:

The chief executive or his representative (chairman)
Heads of departments that are or will be using the computer
The data processing manager

To answer specific questions it may be necessary also to invite:

The systems manager
The programming manager
The operations manager
Computer manufacturer's representative (quarterly)
Consultant's representative (as appropriate)

... check that the people concerned are co-operating

The items on the agenda should cover both projects that are operational on the computer and projects under development.

The data processing manager first reports on how the computer resources have been utilised during the previous month. This report will include both the computer itself and the data preparation and control services. The report should answer questions like: How much of the capacity available is being used on what job? What level of performance is being given to each of the user departments? Any problems experienced with the computer equipment itself are discussed with the manufacturer's representative.

His second report is on progress in each current project and any difficulties encountered. Have there been any significant changes to the system? If so, how do they affect the cost/benefit comparison? How much time has been devoted to every project? Are they ahead of or behind schedule?

His third report is on the maintenance position. How much time has been devoted to modifying and correcting existing systems (this figure may be a big surprise)? How many jobs are being completed each month? What is the backlog of jobs in progress and jobs not yet started?

In this way, the meeting is centred on these main reports and the other people attending are in a position to comment on what is said. The chief executive is able to form his own opinion of progress made and to check that the people concerned are co-operating.

SYSTEMS DEVELOPMENT

The first step in installing computers is the minute examination of the organisation and its work. The job which is going on to the computer must be dissected and systematised to make it suitable for mechanisation, but since both the changed methods and the new approaches will have an impact on the rest of the company, the whole system must be looked at.

This implies asking not just how the work is done but also why. In the process not only will new solutions emerge, but even the original problem may disappear or change so dramatically as to need a totally new approach.

'Systems analysis is associated with that class of problems where the difficulty lies in deciding what ought to be done – not simply how to do it – and honours go to people who find out what the problem is.' (E. S. Quade, *Analysis for Military Decisions.*)

At first sight the task of system design and programming, called *system development* for convenience, seems straightforward enough. The organisation purchases or hires a computer and the managers explain to computer experts what they want it to do. The computer experts then explain how much of what the management wants is feasible and how much the various solutions will cost, and may make a few suggestions of their own. As a result of this process, management makes an informed decision on what the computer is to do, and the computer experts buckle down to the task of getting the computer to do it.

As you might expect, it just does not happen that way and the description would bring a sour smile to the face of any executive who has been involved with systems development. What seems at first a perfectly straightforward and logical process turns out to be almost always quite extraordinarily difficult and taxing, and the complexity often takes people by surprise.

A manager who bought a computer for sales accounting once came to us very puzzled. The computer manufacturer's proposal was simple, straightforward, easily understood and it occupied about six pages. He bought the computer and the systems analysts designed the system in detail and prepared a specification for the programmers to work from. This was a document of some 600 pages, highly complex, not at all straightforward and very difficult to understand. 'What', asked the manager, 'has happened? Why has something essentially so simple turned into something so complex?'

The point is that most computer systems are simple enough in outline, but they get loaded with a great mass of exceptions and special cases. **The straightforward explanation of the system leaves out 95 per cent of the problem.** The complex but comprehensive explanation is, on the other hand, a tough proposition.

Getting a computer to do a useful job does not present technical difficulties – the problem is not in the programming. If the company is using tried and tested hardware and has no fancy peripherals attached, the main problem is specifying the jobs.

Surprisingly **it turns out to be easier to formulate the equations required to put man on the moon than it is to specify invoicing in a form suitable for a computer.** Even a salary system can take twelve man months to specify – and salary work is a comparatively simple and well understood application.

This is also partly the reason we need systems analysts; managers lack the analytical training required to specify their needs and cannot in any case spare the time, so unfortunately we must extend the communications chain with specialists.

For engineers and others with 'problem solving' applications, computer 'languages' (notably FORTRAN and BASIC) have been developed which correspond closely to algebra. These languages allow the man with the problem to program the solution himself. This is a much more satisfactory arrangement.

Attempts have also been made to construct languages that will enable the manager to program business data processing applications directly. These have been relatively unsuccessful because, as we have seen, the biggest hurdle lies in formulating the problem (a hurdle the 'problem solver' does not have to overcome). It seems the systems analyst and the programmer will be needed by the business manager for a long time to come.

Writing computer programs is relatively simple. Programmers are often wildly optimistic on job timing, but though dislocation of the commissioning schedule is serious, it is comparatively unusual for programmers to fail completely to produce the required programs.

To see that the harder part is specifying the problem rather than programming it, one has only to see businesses where the computer is an admitted failure. You would think the computer would be standing idle for most of the day, either because it had broken down, or because it had no work to do. In fact the computer is usually desperately overloaded and working all round the clock. Furthermore, the computer programs may be extremely efficiently written; they do the work they are designed for in the shortest possible time. The programs do efficiently what the computer experts intended but they do not serve the needs of the business; the tool is being used for the wrong job. **Even genius at the technical level cannot compensate for design failure.**

For example, in one company we were told by the data processing manager, 'We have a wonderful sales statistics system here – three miles of paper every week.' Further investigation showed that most of this huge report was pushed into various filing systems, was never looked at and was eventually discarded. Even the parts of the report used did not present the information in a suitable way, and further work had to be done by clerks before it could be used. There was no technical failure here at all; the programmers and computer operators were competent and conscientious; the trouble was that the computer was simply not doing a useful job.

The chief problems, therefore, in developing computer systems arise before the programming stage is reached. They are concerned with getting a decision on exactly *what* the computer is to do.

Unfortunately, a great deal of so-called computer education for managers places the emphasis wrongly. Indeed, much of it is little more than training in elementary computer programming. There are various reasons for this bias. Programming is an interesting subject in its own right and some slight acquaintance with it is probably quite useful to managers. Furthermore, it is a very teachable subject; it is a clear body of knowledge and is consequently popular with teachers. Finally, since much computer education is in the hands of computer manufacturers, they naturally concentrate on their own machines and programming languages.

Although this kind of technical education has value for the manager it can be positively misleading if it makes the manager think that the only, or even the principal, problems are technical – i.e. in the programming.

Before starting the job of analysing the existing systems and discussing new ones, one must identify appropriate application areas and priorities for improvement, and these can only be determined by some sort of preliminary survey by managers, perhaps with help from systems analysts. Once managers have decided which application areas are to be studied first, it is time to call in the systems analyst to carry out the detailed investigation.

That involves:

1. Surveying the existing and desired system

2. Evaluating alternative methods for improving the system

3. Specifying the manual and computer procedures to be adopted

After that comes the programming of the computer procedures and finally implementation.

The system must be reviewed to ensure the promised benefits are achieved and to learn from mistakes. In practice, the preliminary survey to detect application areas and priorities for improvement should be a continuous activity and the audit of previous applications should form a part of it.

Basic Project Stages	*The Five-Stage Approach*
Diagnosis Stage	1. Surveying the existing system
Creative Stage	2. Evaluating alternative methods for improvement
Implementation Stage . .	3. Specifying the new manual and computer procedures
	4. Programming the computer procedures
	5. Implementing the new system

FIG. 23 Systems Analysis

It has been found necessary to divide the task of systems analysis into clearly defined stages – both as an aid to the systems analyst (providing a framework for a systematic approach) and to his manager (providing a method for both scheduling and control).

SURVEYING THE SYSTEM

The process of analysis starts with a look at existing procedures across the whole organisation, not just the part to be put on the computer. This will establish orderly working and mesh the new methods with what remains of the old. This sort of reorganisation and detailed examination must be completed before any programming can start.

Invariably, introducing a computer leads to new ways of doing the job; operations that were performed at somebody's discretion are now reduced to rules; there is a need for very accurate clerical work, though there may be an overall reduction in clerical staff employed.

At the survey stage the systems analyst is trying to find out what is happening at present and why, whether it is really necessary, to identify areas of weakness, to discover and identify what else is needed from the system.

In one food distribution system being investigated, the analyst noted that a copy of the customer's order was being used to control delivery failures. Further investigation revealed that customers always telephoned to complain of non-delivery before the office control system had time to react. Cutting out this one procedure saved five clerks and the extra copy on every order, with no loss of service.

This example illustrates the continuing need for the analyst to question what is being done. There are no prizes awarded for solving the wrong problem (however brilliantly) and the survey stage provides the opportunity to stand back and appraise the existing procedures. Distinguish between:

the problem as originally given

the real problem and constraints as revealed by analysis

the part of the problem which is soluble – not all of it may be, at least economically, and a small portion, say 20 per cent, may produce 80 per cent of the needed improvement.

One of the problems of devising a computer system is that there is a need to get the system completely defined before it becomes operational, and indeed before it is programmed. Any errors or omissions are expensive and difficult to rectify later.

This contrasts strongly with clerical systems and, in any case, involves a method of working that is highly unnatural. People prefer to work on a trial and error basis, to 'play it by ear' as they say. Using clerks, a system is roughed out, a few forms and procedures are designed and the job is performed for a few months. As weaknesses are discovered they are corrected; a form may be redesigned or a new colour may be introduced into a colour-coding system. Of course, the system should be designed reasonably correctly in the first place, but there is no pressing need to get every detail right before it becomes operational.

When the management of a company is asked by its systems analysts to consider a computer system for doing a job, it is essentially asked to buy a product which it has not yet seen, which is just a design. This unfortunate state of affairs is quite inevitable at present; implementing computer systems is so time-consuming and so expensive that it is economically impractical to develop a computer system on a trial and error basis.

In practice, this means that every attempt must be made to foresee all possible difficulties before they arise. Furthermore, **managers will have to make very considerable efforts if they are to understand what they are asked to agree to.** It must be emphasised that this process requires time, thought and imagination, but it is essential if a satisfactory system is to be implemented.

In addition, there is the problem of keeping the computer system up to date. No business remains static for very long. At one end of the scale it is constantly making minor changes to, say, the products, the product range, the prices and the discount structure. At the other end of the scale it is making major changes, attempting to penetrate new markets, opening new depots and new factories. So it is wise to allow for ease of change in the computer.

A computer program for printing invoices, for instance, has to read the quantities different customers have ordered of different products, and multiply each by the appropriate price to obtain the value of the order. It is perfectly possible to build into the computer program itself the product code and the price of each product. Possible, but not very practical, because the program would have to be changed every time a product was added to the range or the price of a product altered. Since modifying programs takes time and costs money, it is best avoided where possible.

The alternative solution is to arrange for the price list to be stored outside the program. One method is to keep the price list punched on a file of cards. These cards are read by the program every time invoices are to be printed. Now, if there is a price change, it is a simple clerical procedure to replace the present card for a product with another. The program itself stays the same – it merely uses the revised price list. Alternatively the price list can be stored on magnetic tape or disc. This is safer, more secure and in some ways more convenient, but more expensive, and it needs a special program to change the prices – magnetic media, unlike cards, cannot be corrected by hand.

Giving flexibility to a computer system ensures that it is not always necessary to change the programs when the needs of the business change.

There are, however, changes which can only be made by changing the program. Suppose that the pricing policy changes so that in future different prices are to be charged for the same product in different areas. The price list, which before looked like this:

PRODUCT	PRICE IN PENCE
A	11
B	8
C	11
D	15
.	. .
.	. .

now looks like this:

PRODUCT	PRICE IN PENCE *Area 1*	*Area 2*	*Area 3*
A	11	12	11
B	8	9	8
C	11	12	11
D	15	17	15
	..	..	..

It will not be possible for the computer to apply this new price structure until a good deal of re-programming has been done because we did not tell it originally that prices could depend on area as well as product, and so it was not in the original instructions. If this change had been foreseen, it would have been possible to build the capability into the program in the first place.

However, nobody can foresee all the possible changes and in any case it would not be feasible to enable the program to cope with everything that might ever possibly happen.

It is possible to construct a system that is, within limits, very flexible indeed. Unfortunately, outside these limits, there is no flexibility; changes in requirements have to be met by time-consuming and expensive re-programming.

Flexibility is one of the basic problems in the business use of computers. The problem can be eased by insisting that programmers keep records and annotate their programs to make change easier (at the moment they often fail to do so). Furthermore, intelligent forward thinking at the design stage can often predict future changes. Most valuable of all, arrangements should be made to give system designers and programmers as much advance warning as possible of impending changes.

There is no complete solution. In a typical computer installation, it is commonplace to discover that 25 per cent of the system designers' and programmers' time is taken up with maintaining existing systems instead of developing new ones. **Certainly, if major unpredictable changes are liable to happen in any area of the business, then that area is probably not suitable for the use of a computer** (Chapter 2 again).

In a way it is odd that computers have become associated in people's minds with change – the idea that computers are for thrusting, dynamic companies that are penetrating new markets, developing new products, acquiring subsidiaries and so on. In fact, computers operate best in stable situations, where procedures change only slowly and only in minor ways. It is possible to put up the paradoxical argument (we would not want to be taken too seriously when we state it) that **thrusting, dynamic companies ought to leave computers alone until they become old and staid.**

EVALUATING ALTERNATIVE SOLUTIONS

It is the manager's job to ensure that evaluation covers alternative solutions, including improvements to the present system, that do not entail a computer.

A common danger is that the simple (and often effective) solution is excluded, mainly because it is easier to understand its implications and so it is easier to see where it is likely to fail. The more complex solutions are accepted because they are not really understood by the manager, nor are their implications.

We once carried out an experiment with fifteen experienced middle managers. They were asked to think about the areas for improvement in a given situation. They then received a presentation in which three alternative solutions were put forward:

an improved manual system

a part manual, part computer system

a fully integrated computer system

In the discussions which followed, the first (manual) system was heavily criticised for its shortcomings, the second received some criticism (more questions than criticisms) but, for the third – no comments. When all questions and discussions had stopped, the managers were asked to select the most promising system. All but two selected the third.

But the third was the most complex system, the one they understood least and the one about which they had asked no questions. And, as you might expect, the second and third solutions also had quite as many shortcomings as the first.

The lesson to be learned is that you may well be tempted to take an unwise course because you cannot see the problems. **Beware of introducing systems you do not fully understand.**

And, we repeat, an important point to remember is that computers may turn out not to be the most practicable answer. Without managerial involvement it is all too easy for analysts to fall into the trap of saying 'Here is the computer, now where are the problems?', rather than 'What are the problems, and do we need a computer to solve them?' For example:

In a manufacturing company a computer was used to analyse market trends. As part of a study to evaluate alternative methods it was discovered that the job could be done sufficiently reliably by taking a random sample. The job was taken off the computer and done by the existing clerical staff in twenty minutes each day which was twenty-four hours faster, and significantly cheaper.

Another reason to look very hard at computer options is that bringing in the equipment may introduce new problems of its own.

A motor supplier we know transferred records for 20,000 stock items from a handwritten stock ledger on to a computer. A main advantage of the change was the computer's ability to read through the stock records every few days and print a list of items out of stock or about to be out of stock. This could obviously not have been done so quickly and frequently on the old method without an enormous number of extra clerks.

But previously an enquiry about a stock item required only looking at the appropriate ledger page, and since there were only about ten of these enquiries each day, they did not seriously disrupt the work of posting new receipts and issues to the ledger.

Computer records cannot be looked at in the same simple way and a special program had to be prepared to read a list of item numbers, about which details were requested, and scan the file, printing details of the items in question. Since this program took at least thirty minutes to run, it was obviously impossible to disrupt the computer's work schedule every time an enquiry came along. Enquiries were restricted to one run a day so all enquiries received by noon were processed as a batch. This meant that an enquiry took at least an hour to answer (thirty minutes for the computer run plus thirty minutes for card punching, etc.) and in the worst case could take twenty-four hours or more to answer. In consequence, the service provided by the computer was in some respects very much worse than that provided by the previous system, and the computer was soon in bad odour amongst at least some of the managers.

Of course, the issue is more complicated than it seems here. The question might be raised of whether all these enquiries were really necessary or whether they could be answered by some document printed by the computer on a routine basis. However, the fact is that designers of computer systems have to exercise a great deal of ingenuity to overcome the unfortunate fact that a computer's central records are not immediately accessible.

At this point, a computer expert may accuse us of being technically out of date since it would be possible to store the records on magnetic disc, not tape. So whenever an item number was typed in at the console, the computer could flash back details of the item on to the screen of a VDU within a second or two.

Of course, this is true. Unfortunately, it would be likely to add significantly to the cost of most computers. In many circumstances this kind of enquiry system is justified, but even so it would be a lot more expensive than the clerical enquiry system, which cost almost nothing, and the cost would have to be recovered by economies in other areas.

The main point is this: **computers do not produce benefits right across the board. Any computer system is likely to have elements in it which are far clumsier and more expensive than the corresponding elements in the system that it replaces.** There may have to be some fairly radical thinking about the way the business round the computer operates; certainly **it is not realistic to think of the computer as a new gadget for doing the same old job.**

It is this that makes managers ask indignantly: 'Do you seriously mean to tell us that we are to reorganise our business merely to suit the convenience of your wretched computer?' The answer is no – and yes. Clearly, any machine which radically changes the economics of doing a job should make you think about the job itself. For example, developments in machine tools have radically affected many companies' patterns of business; they now make different products. Similarly, the advent of computers may make an organisation modify its methods of working, or lead to the formation of new organisations.

To summarise, computers constantly introduce new cost/effectiveness considerations into a business, and in many cases they will lead management to modify the services that they offer to their customers or the procedures to be used by their own staff. The key point is that such decisions must be made by management, and not by the computer staff, who are likely to have their own technological axe to grind.

When evaluating alternatives:

compare the cost for the same degree of effectiveness

compare the relative effectiveness of the same cost

We should also be interested in the Pareto principle – look for the 80 per cent benefit that can be achieved with 20 per cent of the effort.

And when you have got an answer but have difficulty estimating development costs, remember that computer service bureaux whose livelihood depends on accurate estimates and controlled costs are a useful guide. They can estimate a time and a price for your projects and, if they can do it, so must your own computer staff.

Here is another case study to try your hand at. It is a heavily disguised example taken from an actual company – see how your ideas and conclusions compare with ours.

CASE STUDY 3 – MARIE CORMACK S.A.

BACKGROUND

Marie Cormack is organised into two divisions. The larger division (turnover about £10 million) manufactures and sells a standard range of cosmetics under the brand name 'Marie'. The smaller division (turnover £5 million) manufactures 'own brand' cosmetics, soaps, etc. for other companies to sell under their own house name – usually one-off products in fairly small batches.

The cost of order processing and invoicing in the smaller 'Specials Division' is thought to be high and in addition the average debt (accounts receivable) is fifteen weeks. Management is thought to be weak, and recently the administration manager was fired and replaced by another man.

The situation in the larger 'Cosmetics Division' is much better. They have a successful computer installation which is carrying out order processing, stock control, invoicing and sales ledger. There are no current computer applications in the Specials Division.

Two of the computer systems analysts from Cosmetics have been asked to carry out a survey of the problems of Specials and to recommend improvements.

SYSTEMS RECOMMENDATIONS

The areas giving trouble are order processing, invoicing and sales ledger. The existing activities and clerical staff are:

	Clerical staff	*Volumes*
Quotations	2	5,000 p.a.
Order acknowledgement	2	10,000 p.a.
Invoicing (weekly)	3	25,000 p.a.
Sales ledger	2	600 customers

The systems report said:

1. The existing systems are unsatisfactory, with many errors and queries. There is also some evidence of overstaffing.

2. It would be possible to use the Cosmetics computer to integrate the systems, capturing the basic data from the quotation and using it for order acknowledgement, invoicing and sales ledger.

3. There is ample capacity for the job on the Cosmetics computer and satisfactory turnround could be provided.

4. The cost justification study shows the project is very cost effective. Points mentioned include:

   the computer is costless, as savings made in Cosmetics are paying the rental it would be possible to adapt the existing Cosmetics computer programs to suit Specials' requirement

it is likely there will be a reduction in the existing staff numbers

5. It would be possible to take on this work within the next six months.

WHAT IS YOUR VERDICT?

The systems report recommends moving to a computer system to overcome the problems of Specials. In addition, the new administration manager is in favour. What is your verdict?

(*a*) Accept the recommendations
(*b*) Accept with some misgivings (what?)
(*c*) Reject the recommendations
(*d*) Postpone a decision
(*e*) Don't know

Decide what you would do before reading on.

MARIE CORMACK SOLUTION

The great cost justification illusion
The systems men have made out a very plausible case:

a computer available with idle time

systems and programs largely developed

the possibility of staff savings

the promise of overcoming the present problems

Most managers would accept with alacrity – but they would later regret their enthusiasm. The systems men have fallen into a number of common traps.

First, they have compared the existing badly run sloppy manual system with an idealistic computer system. They should also have considered how best to improve the manual system (which is grossly overstaffed to get out 500 or so invoices per week). They have ignored the rule: **always evaluate alternative ways of improving the system.**

Second, it is bad practice to transfer a poor manual system to a computer. The present staff is undisciplined and error prone, yet a computer requires rigid discipline and absolute accuracy. **They should consider the potential for improving the existing system before considering a computer.**

Third, it looks as though the system is input dominated and will be uneconomic – even if the computer time is free. The job is not one of invoicing a standard range of products with high volumes; it is invoicing special lines (special prices, special descriptions) with low volumes. The cost of input to the computer may exceed an efficient manual system. **Input-dominated applications do not usually make good computer applications.**

Fourth, the proposal used evocative words to cloud the validity of the recommendations:

'free computer time'	marginal pricing of computer time anyway is unwise
'integrate the systems'	a sharp pencil and carbon paper would achieve the same result
'adapt existing programs'	adapting programs which have not been designed with flexibility in mind is a messy and time-consuming task, usually underestimated

VERDICT

Reject the recommendations. Then go and see the systems manager to see what he plans to do to broaden the perspective of his staff.

CLERICAL RULES AND REALITY

When we devise rules for doing a business job, these rules tend, for very good reasons, to be extremely complex. As we have seen, this fact is observed because very often businesses do not devise rules at all, or when they do they are only a general guide to action and are not intended to be complete.

Where rules and procedures are formulated and written down, the result is extreme verbosity and complexity. Consider the Army Pay Manual, which is essentially the rules for paying soldiers. This is a very large book about 4 inches (100 mm) thick, doing what might seem to be a very simple job. One's first reaction is that it is needlessly lengthy and involved, but in fact there is hardly a word wasted in it.

We have already given some idea of the way specifications are reached and the criteria they should meet. Once all the rules have been made explicit and all the alternatives considered, the task is probably already halfway specified. But filling in the details can be a complex task.

We and our subordinates use greater range of discretionary power than is readily apparent, but before the computer can cope all this discretion must be reduced to rules. If you think this is simple, consider the example a few pages further on of compiling nothing more elaborate than a sorted list of customer names. Evolving specifications is a long, tough job and needs care.

A company was using a computer for producing sales invoices and statements, and for maintaining the sales ledger. Each month a statement was printed for each customer with a credit and debit balance. One copy was despatched to him and another copy was given to the collection department.

The collection department watched the customer's account, sent reminders if he failed to pay, and ultimately stopped his credit and took legal action if the debt became seriously overdue. The department was understaffed and overworked and, in consequence, a great many customers were being allowed to run up larger and larger debts. The question was raised of whether the job could be taken over by the computer, using it to print standard reminder and demand letters. Obviously the first task was to establish the rules and procedures that were being followed at the time. In theory, no action was taken until the customer had received a second monthly statement. Then, if he failed to pay within fourteen days, a reminder letter was sent. After a further fourteen days a final reminder was sent and legal proceedings instituted after a further week.

These theoretical rules were hardly ever followed in practice. A customer often refused to pay because there was a query concerning some of the goods supplied – he might be dissatisfied with their quality or he might claim not to have received them. In these cases no further action was taken until the dispute had been resolved by the sales department. If only a part of the debt was in dispute the customer was asked to pay the part about which there was no dispute. The collection manager also used his discretion and his knowledge of the customer.

A gentleman's agreement had come about under which it was understood that a large number of important customers received more generous credit terms than the others. In practice, they were being given approximately nine months' credit.

There was also a class of customers designated VIPs, and if one of these had a debt more than three months old, the collection department simply told the managing director who made a personal approach to the customer concerned. Unfortunately, the number of VIPs had increased over the years to over 150 customers, and at any one time about fifty had debts that were more than three months old. These debts accounted for some 15 per cent of the total owed by all customers.

Finally, the theoretical rules were not followed in practice because of staff shortages within the collection department. As the manager said, 'These aren't so much rules as targets we set ourselves; in fact, I very much doubt whether it would be in the company's interests to follow these rules to the letter, even if we could. In our kind of business, if we chase our customers too hard, they will go to some other supplier who will give them more generous terms.'

What the investigation showed, therefore, was that:

1. The rules were not being followed in practice.

2. The rules were incomplete, in the sense that much was left to somebody's discretion.

3. What was being done in practice was admittedly not ideal – the

methods had developed in a haphazard way over a number of years.

4. It was not clear that it would be in the interests of the business strictly to enforce such rules as there were.

The investigation and design process took several months, and in the end an agreed set of rules for debt collection was formulated. It was decided to divide the customers into three classes:

1. A greatly reduced number of VIPs.

2. 'Generous term' customers, who were allowed to take three months' credit.

3. Normal customers, who were allowed to take two months' credit.

Detailed rules were set up for dealing with cases where there was a query on the account, and the procedure was ultimately transferred to the computer.

This instance, which is absolutely typical, illustrates two important points. Firstly, it is, strictly speaking, **impossible to transfer a clerical system to a computer; the computer system will always be different from the clerical system that it replaces.** These differences are quite likely to involve important points of company policy. Therefore, the transfer of work to a computer cannot be left entirely to the computer staff. Formulating rules to replace management discretionary powers is a job that must involve management.

When transferring a job to a computer, it is inevitable that one should take a critical look at the job itself. In this case, it was obvious that the system for dealing with VIP customers, which was once quite sensible, had become less and less effective. Although it is desirable that the computer staff should make proposals in this area, they should not be allowed to take decisions, nor should management merely rubber-stamp their recommendations.

A corollary of this is that, **since the computer system is nearly always different from the system it replaces, it is by no means easy to estimate the benefits brought by the computer – the very fact of sys-**

tematisation increases efficiency. In the case we have been discussing, in the six months following the change to the computer system, the total debt dropped from £400,000 to £300,000, although sales revenue had remained constant. In a sense, this drop was due to the computer, but the question should still be asked: how much could the debt have been reduced by an improved clerical system? And at what cost?

In fact, one of the tricks of the computer man's trade is to take some inefficient clerical system which has been allowed to decay for years. He replaces it by a moderately efficient computer system and can demonstrate gigantic savings, which he then attributes to the computer and his genius.

Chapter 6

Implementation

Once the systems analysts have found what the job is to be done and how it should be tackled, more detailed rules and methods for computerisation are evolved before programming can begin. Throughout this process managers must still watch the project control problems, and as the implementation phases in, will find the human aspect taking on increasing importance.

SPECIFYING THE MANUAL AND COMPUTER PROCEDURES

Before the systems analyst carries on to specify the procedures in detail, management authorisation to proceed is required. So far, the company has been committed to perhaps a few months' survey and evaluation work from a trained systems analyst. In most cases this survey will show areas where short-term improvements can be made in the existing system, so such surveys should be at least self-financing. But once the decision is taken to 'go' with a computer system the cost begins to rise and the decision proves very difficult to reverse.

In one large manufacturing company which was heavily dependent on a computer, the consultants appraising the computer performance looked for those occasions where the senior management had formally taken decisions regarding its introduction and use. Only one positive decision was found: to authorise the initial feasibility study. The study presumably gathered momentum and the project was assumed to continue – the machine was ordered and staff recruited without a decision from senior management.

Assuming the manager is satisfied that the proposal satisfies a genuine business need, *there are certain technical questions he must address to the data processing manager:*

Why have you recommended this solution rather than any other?

Are you absolutely certain the computer can handle the job in the way you say and in the time you say? Which is the most critical area?

Are you absolutely certain the user department staff have the ability to carry out their new tasks and that your timing estimates are sufficiently generous? Where are the bottlenecks likely to be?

Are you prepared to be held to your man-day and cost estimates?

Is this project similar to something we have done before? If not, should we not get an outside specialist to review our proposal (the only possible answer is 'Yes, we do need a second opinion')?

Do we have adequate standby in the event of machine failure?

By asking these questions you are making the data processing manager put his reputation on the line and you are genuinely giving him a chance to reconsider any possibly rash promises.

Assuming agreement is given to proceed, the next stage is to produce a precise specification of requirements. During this specification stage the systems analyst must specify both the manual and the computer procedures to be adopted. Experience shows that this is best done using carefully thought-out standard documentation as this allows a structured approach to solving the problem, easier communication between staff, less vulnerability from staff turnover and, in particular, a method of controlling the amount of work done.

DETAILED DEFINITIONS OF THE TASK

Before a job can be put on to a computer it must be reduced to a set of completely watertight rules. These detailed rules must anticipate any situations that can possibly arise and must be built into the programs the computer is given right at the start.

It is vital that managers check and understand the specification before programming starts. This is, however, surprisingly difficult even with good documentation because what managers look for tends not to be what systems analysts get wrong. For example:

In a payroll application, the manager would look closely into the specification of a complex bonus calculation – because it is complex. The systems analyst, however, is much more likely to have made a simple type of error – such as not paying a man who is absent. This is because the systems analyst lacks detailed knowledge of the job and has blind spots.

Specifying manual procedures is a neglected but important task for the systems analyst. He must strike a balance between assuming some knowledge of the old job, some application of common sense and the need to provide a reference manual for new staff.

The computer knows only what you tell it. Workers come to you with a background of knowledge, experience and common sense, so a task to be performed by them can get under way with far less preparation. They may sometimes be given complete sets of rules to cover any eventuality, but it is far more likely that they will be given only a few general principles, which they are left to apply at their discretion. In practice, we tend to underestimate the extent to which we leave things to people's discretion.

An example will illustrate this.

A business establishes a card index of customers' names and addresses built up over the years in a fairly informal way. A customer's name might be recorded as:

Mr. J. Hughes
Mr John Hughes
J. Hughes Esq.
etc. etc.

If the card trays are dropped and all the cards are mixed up it would be a fairly simple, though tedious, job to sort the customers back into alphabetical order. Actually, it would not be quite as simple as might at first appear. For example, in some cases, it would be necessary to deviate from strict alphabetical order. It would probably be a good idea to sort Mac and Mc surnames together, as in the telephone directory, so that the order would be:

MacDonald
McDonald
MacEwan

McEwan
M'Ewan
MacPherson
McPherson

and not:

MacDonald
MacEwan
MacPherson
McDonald
McEwan
McPherson
M'Ewan

Double-barrelled surnames would also be a problem: should Lloyd-George be under L or G? It is even possible that there would be a few treble-barrelled names, like Twisleton-Wykeham-Fiennes.

Some surnames of foreign origin would need a decision. Van Dyck would presumably come under V, and de Courcy under D. But there could be two opinions about d'Olivier; should it come under D or O?

However, all these problems are trivial, at least in the sense that they could be delegated to a junior employee. Any intelligent and moderately well educated clerk could sort out the cards into a 'sensible' order without being given detailed instructions.

Now suppose that we gave it to a man who was familiar with our alphabet, but who could not speak English, had never lived in Britain and had no knowledge of our society or its conventions. Such a man would need enormously precise and detailed instructions. For a start, he would have to be told that Mr, Mrs, Miss, Esq., Lord, Lady, Sir, The Revd, Captain, General, and a host of other words were in fact titles and should be ignored for sorting purposes. He might also have to grapple with names like:

The Dean of Westminster
The Duke of Norfolk
Lord George-Brown

One possible simplification would be to tell our clerk to pick out the last word in each name as a first step in sorting:

The Dean of *Westminster*
John *Smith*
The Revd F. *Brown*

He would still, however, need to be told about titles like:

Sir John Smith, Bart.

or Sir John would be sorted under B. But what will happen then to Lionel Bart? In addition, our clerk might be confused by degrees and decorations:

John Smith, D.S.O.
Ian Brown, M.A.

Even initials would present some problems. He could quickly be taught ordinary initials:

G for George, Gavin, etc.
D for David, Daniel, etc.

but he would have trouble with, say:

St J. for St John
D'A. for D'Arcy

What all this means is that a very simple-seeming instruction, 'Sort these names into alphabetical order', is a great deal less simple than it seems. It is only carried out sensibly because the clerk brings to his job a great deal of common sense and general knowledge.

Computers have no common sense or general knowledge, so devising a set of rules that would enable a computer to sort names into sequence is even more complicated and time-consuming than devising rules for the foreign clerk.

To show just how time-consuming detailing such apparently simple tasks can be: it took a very experienced man a complete week to formulate the rules for sorting names in sufficient detail for programming to begin.

There are also practical restrictions on the length and number of names. It may be assumed that no name will consist of more than sixteen letters, and that nobody will have more than four names. Inevitably, this means that in certain (one hopes very rare) cases, abbreviations will be necessary.

Actually, this is an elementary example of one of the systems designer's perennial problems. To the non-specialist, he often seems to be obsessed by questions beginning 'What is the largest possible number of... ?' For example, 'What is the largest number of different delivery addresses a customer can have?' or 'What is the largest number of different processes that can be involved in a single job?' The reason is that when designing forms and allocating computer storage, he constantly has to allow for the worst case, but if he allows too much, the result is a clumsy and inefficient system.

PROGRAMMING THE COMPUTER PROCEDURES

Programming the computer procedures is not normally carried out by the systems analyst, although it may be in the smaller company and for certain specialised applications (for example, R & D projects, and 'real time' systems), and managers will not be much involved.

The main function of the systems analyst at the programming stage is to provide system test data for trial runs and to resolve queries.

PROGRAMMERS

The job of the programmer is first to plan how best the computer should tackle the jobs in the systems specification, and then to write and test the necessary computer programs to ensure it carries out these jobs correctly. This means there are two quite distinct functions: the strategic programmer and the programmer.

In the early days of programming, the two tasks were not distinguished between, which resulted in both waste and inefficiency. Highly qualified and able programmers were required to carry out routine coding while unqualified and junior programmers were allowed to decide the overall strategy for their own programs. It has been found necessary in practice to separate these two tasks so that the right skill is used in the right place.

The job of the strategic programmer

The strategic programmer plans the programs. To do this he needs to understand both how the system is to be used and how it will interact with other systems and procedures. The strategic programmer therefore needs to be involved in the early stages of the systems evaluation and specification.

This can be arranged by adopting the project team approach where the users, systems analysts, strategic programmer and operations manager, pool their skills to arrive at the best combined solu-

... unqualified and junior programmers were allowed to decide the overall strategy for their own programs

tion. Notice that, in a small application, strategic programming is a role, not a full-time job.

The job of the programmer

Once the strategic programmer has analysed the systems specification, designed the computer system and specified the programs, detailed programming can commence. The programming function is managed best by dividing the job into stages, as we did for the job of the systems analyst, so that the work can be timed and controlled by these stages. As a further step, programs should be carefully structured and written in 'modules'.

The basic idea behind 'modular programming' is that it is relatively easy to write and test a small program of 100 instructions. It is much more than ten times as difficult to write and test a program of 1000 instructions without making mistakes. So if a large program is broken down into modules, it should be easier to get the job done.

As a further step the modular structure of the program should logically match the structure of the problem to be solved. For example, in an inventory control program it should be possible to identify separately the modules concerned with:

processing the inventory record
processing each movement record
processing a reorder request

A program structured in this way relates closely to the problem to be solved which makes it easier to understand and to change when the problem changes.

IMPLEMENTING THE NEW SYSTEM

At the implementation stage the systems analyst organises staff training, sets up files required for the new system, tests the new system thoroughly and supervises parallel runs with the old. The manager is also vitally concerned at this stage. One of the marks of the successful system is that the user manager wants to implement it. The new system stands or falls by the ability of the manager's staff to perform the necessary clerical routines, and it is hoped he will have considered this aspect when evaluating alternative methods.

THE HUMAN ASPECT

The installation of a computer involves fairly substantial changes in an organisation, as must by now be obvious. The methods of work, the organisational structure and the work content will all be different, and there will be some staff leaving or made redundant, and new types of staff being taken on. All this will be disruptive, may be uncomfortable and can be seen as threatening; so a whole new set of social tensions may build up.

Some workers may have their roles downgraded, or may see their new tasks as inferior in prestige, intellectual demands or dignity. It may be less pleasant for instance merely to feed information to the computer rather than to do the work.

The company managers may see the new system as unhelpful, obstructive or threatening, especially if they have not been involved in designing and agreeing. They may react with passive non-co-operation; they may blame the computer for every subsequent problem; in very extreme cases, they may even use devious means to defeat the system.

Computer staff, too, may be a cause of resentment. They are fairly expensive specialists who do not fit into existing career, pay or responsibility structures. Their undue weight and salaries can cause resentment. This will be exacerbated by the fact that computer people may not see the company as necessarily their main promotion route.

All this will not endear them to user managers whose lives have been disrupted, whose established jobs have been changed, and whose role may have diminished; especially if the managers feel they will be left carrying the can when the computer man has moved on. The computer people may also tend to look on the rest of the company as dim, unco-operative, and conservative, while themselves being regarded as idle and arrogant boffins ignorant of business problems.

Such problems sometimes arise and they may be to some degree inevitable, but it is senior management's job to prevent them from harming the organisation. If reconciliation fails, it goes without saying that the chances of success are negligible.

Finally, never forget that people tend to resent dealing with machines where they have learned to expect people. This applies to managers, staff and customers. It worries them and displeases them – they cannot negotiate, plead or compromise with a computer, and they cannot charm or bully it. There is a streak of Luddism in most people. Just listen to the anger at the automatic computer bill (and the glee if it is wrong), just hear the dislike of even telephone answering machines.

Probably none of these difficulties can be avoided totally. Intelligent planning though, involvement of people at the planning stage of systems that affect them, sensitivity to human susceptibilities, and plenty of intelligent information, can help minimise them. Explain the reasons for everything, train people, and listen to their grievances and if possible do something about them.

To give you an idea of the sort of problems that come up in practice and how they have to be resolved, here is another of those examples taken from real life (but carefully disguised). See what your verdict would be and how far it tallies with our analysis.

CASE STUDY 4 – LYN TRANSPORT

BACKGROUND

Some years ago the Allied Chemical Group decided to bring together the transport sections of all its subsidiary divisions into a single company – Lyn Transport. Lyn has a head office in the same building as the Allied HQ and thirty depots close to the main manufacturing plants and warehouses throughout the country.

When the transport company was formed, each depot was made a profit centre and encouraged to expand by going outside the group for business. This expansion has proved so successful that about 60 per cent of the work comes from outside the group.

BUSINESS SYSTEMS

Because of the 'jobbing' nature of the work it was decided that estimating and invoicing customers should be done at depot level. This system works well.

A combined estimate/invoice is prepared for each job. The majority of customers do not use Lyn's services more than once a month and so generally pay on the invoice. A small number of regular users, however, receive a monthly statement.

Lyn head office is anxious to minimise the clerical activity at the depots to leave the managers free to concentrate on their primary functions – marketing and transport operations. Accordingly three years ago they decided to prepare centrally the monthly trading accounts for the depots. At about the same time as the centralisation decision was taken, the Allied Group installed a computer at head office so Lyn took advantage of the opportunity to have some of its work carried out on the computer. This now includes purchases, payroll and sales revenue analysis.

For sales revenue analysis a copy of the invoice is used. Every month each branch sends batches of these copy invoices, with the total value of each batch on a control slip, to head office where five full-time clerks write the appropriate revenue class code on each invoice (forty different categories in all, but thirty are rarely used).

The invoices then go to the computer department where the information (mainly invoice totals and revenue class codes) is elaborately checked. When all the batches are correct, the computer prepares a monthly sales revenue analysis by classification by depot. This analysis is then used by Lyn head office staff in the preparation of the trading accounts. A similar procedure is carried out for purchases while the labour costs are derived from the payroll.

The system can be shown schematically as follows:

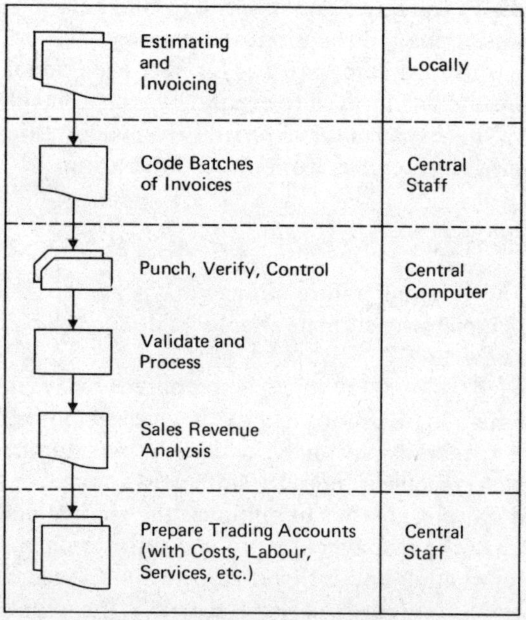

FIG. 24 Paper Flow at Lyn Transport

PRESENT SITUATION

There is general agreement that the present situation is unsatisfactory. The trading accounts appear weeks after the month end and the depot managers dispute the accuracy of the figures.

There is considerable ill-feeling between the Lyn head office staff and the central computer staff. The head office staff blame the computer for the delays and also criticise the way the computer systems were implemented. 'The computer chaps just seemed to lose interest after the pilot depot was taken on. They left us to introduce the system to the other depots which had much greater communications problems.'

The computer staff agree they have made mistakes in the past but say their side is now working well. They are satisfied virtually no errors are made within the computer department. 'Input is the responsibility of Lyn. And you know the old saying: GIGO – Garbage In, Garbage Out.'

WHAT WENT WRONG?

In your opinion what went wrong? In particular:

Have the computer staff failed?
Have the Lyn head office staff failed?
Was the decision to centralise wrong?
Was the decision to use the computer wrong?
Any other comments?

Stop to think and jot down the answers before reading on.

LYN TRANSPORT SOLUTION

The case of Lyn Transport raises a number of points of general interest:

Systems failure: as evidenced by the late and inaccurate trading accounts.

Centralisation or decentralisation: should the invoicing be centralised?

Communications failure

Looking at the systems in more detail:

Local invoicing
Local invoicing for the company appears sensible. A large proportion of the work is 'jobbing' and requires estimates to transient customers. A combined estimate/invoice is both simple and effective.

Central coding
Central coding almost certainly is the major source of errors and misunderstandings. The coding staff are removed from the source of the input, try to guess the correct code in the case of difficulty, and are not motivated to get it right.

Central computer system
The computer system for revenue analysis is highly unsatisfactory. Only one report is produced and that is the sales revenue for each depot analysed under ten main heads. The same result could be achieved by each depot entering its invoices in a book with ten columns (representing analysis heads).

No more work would be required in the depot (they have to add up the invoices now to control the input batches)

The figures could be available weekly, even daily if required, and will not be subject to local dispute

The most obvious benefit of this approach would be to make the five coding clerks unnecessary.

Preparing trading accounts
Replacing the computer system by a local manual system should make it possible to prepare trading accounts faster. But is a month the right time-scale anyway? It is probably right for senior management to monitor depot performance at this interval but depot managers probably need performance measurement in financial terms at least weekly. It is seldom that one report can satisfy the needs of different levels of management.

Centralisation or decentralisation?
As a general rule, centralisation of information flow is inappropriate in situations where local managers have control of local marketing, using local resources in a locally changeable situation. Put another

way, in most situations the shorter and quicker the feedback the better, so local resource decisions tend to be made better locally. While the advance of computers may give the advantages of centralisation with decentralised access, at present this is very rarely achieved.

For example, it has been found that the computer can best assist production planning in an engineering jobbing shop by providing an outline schedule for the coming week, leaving the local management to sequence jobs in the light of the local situation (machine breakdown, material shortage, special labour skills, etc.).

Communications

In an unsuccessful venture it is no surprise to find the two sides blaming each other. Perhaps the most worrying factor is that neither side has thought about how to improve the situation.

What went wrong

Summarising these points:

The computer staff failed to understand what makes a good computer application; they did not fully implement their system; they seem to have lost interest.

The Lyn head office staff were wrong to centralise all accounting work. Centralisation may help the accountants but not the local managers in this case.

The depots had no direct link to the computer department – their information went through the accounts section – and so the data they received from the computer was not what they wanted.

It was wrong to use the computer on the sales revenue analysis application.

Monthly may have been the right interval for central control of profitability, but in this business weekly monitoring is required locally.

The computer men were caught in a power triangle – the *accountants* dreamed up a system for the *computer staff* to foist on the *depot managers*.

The whole system was misconceived and no matter how well executed was bound to bring the computer department into disrepute.

The problems might have been avoided if the managers had been clear on their objectives and if the specialists had considered alternative methods (not just the computer).

INFORMATION INPUT

Yet a further problem, and one which persists throughout the life of the computer, is to ensure that the information going in is accurate.

One approach is to divide documents into batches, typically of 100, and to add up some item, say quantities ordered, and write the total on to a 101st document as control. When the 101 documents have been punched and fed to the computer, it can check the total. If the two totals do not tally, the computer rejects the entire batch. Either a document has been mispunched or – and unfortunately, it is just as likely – the clerk who formed the control total made a mistake.

As an alternative to this method, or as a supplement to it, cards or tapes can be verified. Punched cards are put in the hopper of a second machine which looks like a punch and the operator goes through the motions of punching them again. If the key struck by the operator does not match what is on the card the machine locks and the offending card must be repunched. Paper tape verifiers work on similar principles, though usually a completely new tape is produced. Verification when using key to disc encoders is simpler than either of these, and is one of their chief advantages.

Whether the check-total method, involving an adding machine, or the verification method is used, the result is the same. **For each character or digit that goes into the computer at least two keys have to be struck on some machine or other.** In the interests of accuracy this is quite inevitable.

The cards or tape can now be input to the computer and usually the first program to be run is a checking program.

One of the kinds of check that the computer can perform is the control total check that has already been discussed. There are, though, several other kinds.

First there is range and format checking. For example, in a week, an employee might work for 30, 42, 46 or 52 hours. He could not work for 210 hours (more hours than there are in a week), or XX3A7 hours (it is gibberish).

Therefore, a computer can be programmed to check that the hours punched on a card are, firstly, a number, and secondly, less than, say, 60 (if we can assume that nobody works more than a 59-hour week).

This kind of check is useful for detecting nonsense but, of course, it will not detect plausible errors (for example, 40 instead of 44). Its big advantage is that, although it has to be built into the program, it does not make extra work for the people who prepare the input.

Another much used checking method is modulus checking. For example, when assigning account numbers to customers it might be made a rule that the numbers used must leave no remainder when divided by 9, for example 0081, 9000, 9999, 0270 would all be valid account numbers, but 0083 would not. This is known as modulus 9 checking.

It might be thought therefore that if an error is made, there are eight chances in nine that the computer would detect the mistake. This would be true if mistakes were random, but in practice they are not. For example, as every telephone user knows, transposition errors are very common, e.g. 2070 or 0720 for 0270, and, as a little thought will show, modulus 9 checking is always unable to detect them. For this reason, the modulus checking systems used in practice, although the same in principle, are much more cunning and complicated than this.

A perennial problem in systems for checking the input is how much of the input should be rejected when errors are found.

Suppose that we input 2000 sales orders with several items on each. Obviously it would be absurd for the computer to reject all 2000 orders because there was an error on one. It would be better to print invoices for the 1999 'good' orders and reject just one. In fact, if the error were confined to one item of an order (say, the item code referred to a non-existent item) then it is arguable that the computer should print an invoice for the order omitting only the item on which there was an error.

Unfortunately, this second 'liberal' approach creates control problems; it is difficult to keep track of a lot of small errors that are in the process of being put right. In practice the orders would normally be divided into, say, 20 batches of 100 orders each and the invoices for the whole batch would be delayed until every error had been removed from it. As a result, all the 'good' orders in 'bad' batches would be held up in this annoying way.

Some kind of compromise solution has to be found, but picking a suitable batch size is a major problem.

Batch rejection rates generally vary from about 2 per cent to 20 per cent although in very bad cases some alarming things can happen:

Run 1	Batches:	100	Accepted:	26	Rejected:	74
Re-run 2	Batches:	74	Accepted:	34	Rejected:	40
Re-run 3	Batches:	40	Accepted:	21	Rejected:	19
Re-run 4	Batches:	19	Accepted:	10	Rejected:	9
Re-run 5	Batches:	9	Accepted:	4	Rejected:	5
Re-run 6	Batches:	5	Accepted:	2	Rejected:	3
Re-run 7	Batches:	3	Accepted:	2	Rejected:	1
Re-run 8	Batches:	1	Accepted:	1	Rejected:	0
					Total Rejections:	151

The rejection rate in this case is 151 per cent. This is not a fanciful example; it is drawn from real life and illustrates what will almost certainly happen if the clerical system for correcting errors is ineffective. Note too that several working days probably will elapse before the last batch is accepted.

Even in well-managed installations this recycling of wrong data is a major factor in determining the overall speed of the system, and it is one in which the efficiency of the clerical processes is critical while the speed and power of the computer itself have a relatively trivial effect.

DATA TRANSMISSION

Often the computer is some distance from where the significant events take place. It may be several hundred yards from where goods are produced or issued from stock and it may be hundreds of miles from where sales are made. There are two basic problems: The information must get from the person who first records it to the computer and errors and queries should be sent back.

In the past input documents were physically transported to a data processing centre where the other operations, punching, etc., take place. As a variation, sometimes the information is punched on to

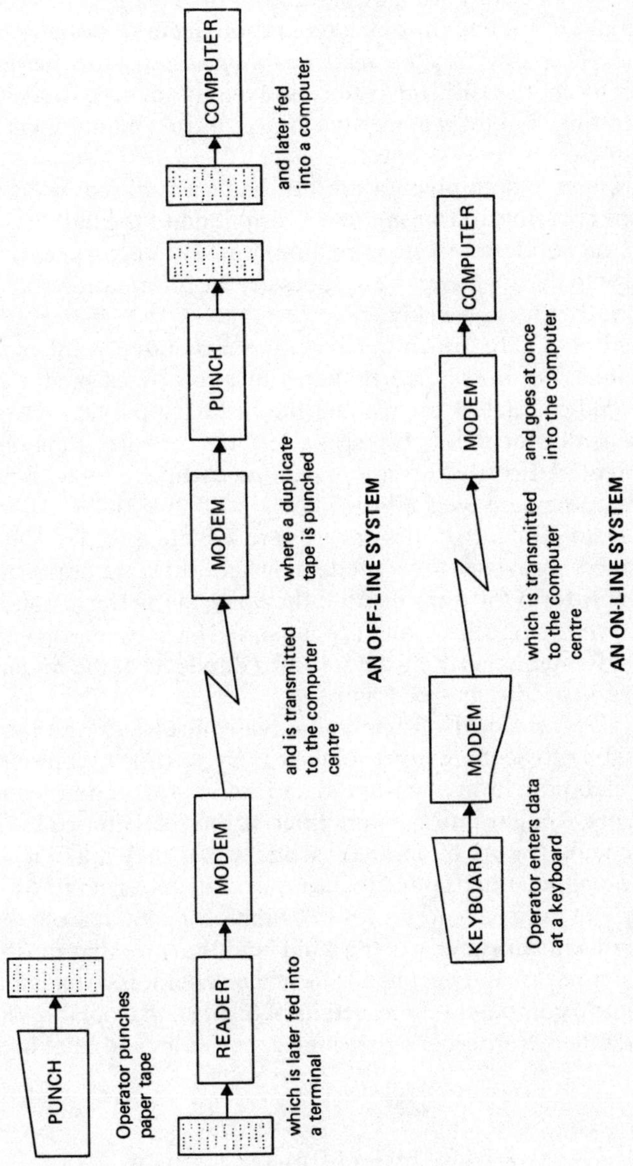

FIG. 25 Data Transmission

tape or cards before being dispatched to the computer. This has the advantage of putting the data preparation operator close to the person who prepares the document, enabling some of the queries to be dealt with more easily. It has the disadvantage of decentralising data preparation, making it more difficult to control and more vulnerable to staff changes and sickness.

However, if data preparation can be decentralised in this way it becomes possible to transmit the information to the data processing centre via public or private telephone lines. Although expensive compared with the postal services, it does get the information to the computer rather more quickly.

The Post Office, which of course has a monopoly, offers a range of services. For the services that operate at a slow or medium speed, up to 200 characters per second, the ordinary public network can be used; but for the higher speed services, private telephone lines are essential. Private lines are sometimes cheaper even with the slow service if they are used a lot.

In its simplest form tapes or cards are fed into a reader; the signals generated are passed to a 'modem', where they are converted into a suitable form for transmission; they pass along the telephone line to the processing centre; they are converted back by another modem; and they enter a punching device and a duplicate of the original tape or card is produced – see Figure 25.

This is often called 'off-line' and is really just a fast (and expensive) alternative to sending tapes and cards by post or by messenger. A more elaborate form is 'on-line' data transmission, and the information goes straight into the computer at the receiving end.

The main feature of on-line systems is that they make it possible for the computer to respond to the input as it comes in piece by piece, and where necessary to return information to the remote location. The best-known systems of this kind (and the ones that most people come across) are the various airline seat reservation systems, in which the central computer retains details of flights and available seats and updates them from second to second as enquiries and bookings come in.

OVERCOMING THE INPUT PROBLEM

There are several ways in which the input process can be simplified, speeded up and made cheaper. It is, above all, an area in which the user departments can make major contributions to the design of the system.

'Exception' input

In one company most of the staff on the weekly payroll worked a standard forty-hour week. On the average, fewer than 5 per cent of the employees worked more or less than this number of hours. The computer was programmed therefore to assume that an employee had worked a forty-hour week unless there was a punched card to indicate the contrary. By this simple device the volume of input was reduced by 95 per cent.

In a sense, all file maintenance operations are examples of exception input. Typically, the computer stores a file of customer details and every week the file is 'updated', that is to say we give input to the computer that tells it how the customer details have changed since last week. There will be details for new customers; old customers may be deleted, or some of their details may be changed.

An interesting example of exception input arose in a company that maintained a chain of shops which it supplied with fast-moving goods by a daily delivery. The obvious way of handling the input would be to make the shop managers telephone their orders each day and to record and punch them in the normal way. However, it became clear on analysis that the pattern of orders was fairly standardised and, although there was great variation from shop to shop and also with the different days of the week, it was possible to establish a standard order for each shop on any day of the week. These standard orders were stored on magnetic tape and the shop managers telephoned only if they wished to vary the order. The system worked well in practice; the only real operational difficulty was that certain managers felt obliged to telephone in a few small variations each day – in case the head office thought they were being idle.

'Turn-around' documents

Customer statements sometimes incorporate a remittance advice in the form of a card, punched by the computer at the time of producing the statement. When returned with the correct payment, the card can be input directly to the system to indicate that the whole debt has been settled. Obviously this method is only appropriate when a considerable proportion of customers remit the exact total shown on the statement, and also return the remittance advice with their payment.

The method can be useful in production control, for when a job is planned the computer punches one card for each stage of the process and these cards are returned, one by one, as each stage is completed.

The great advantage of this method is that it eliminates not just punching and verifying but coding as well, as the computer punches the necessary codes on the card in the first place.

'By-product' input

Sometimes computer input can be produced as the by-product of another process. For example, retail shops often want to input to a computer the information on the tally rolls of their cash registers, and some cash registers will punch paper tape which contains the same information that is on the tally roll. Similarly, some add-listing devices and accounting machines will produce punched tape as a by-product.

By using devices of this kind it is sometimes possible to move to computer processing without substantially increasing the number and scale of keyboard operations.

'Direct' input

One question which is bound to be raised is, 'Why go to all this trouble of punching and verifying tape or cards? Why can't we have some device that can read documents that have been written by a human being?'

A good deal of progress has been made along these lines, but it has been disappointingly slow and the cost of the more elaborate devices, at least, is still extremely high. There are three main kinds of device in this area.

Firstly, there are devices that can read printed or typed (*not* handwritten) characters, either by an optical or by a magnetic sensing process (e.g. the printing along the bottom of most cheques). The advantage here is that the same document can be read by both a computer and a human being. Unfortunately, of course, there is still a printing or typing operation involved and these readers can cost ten times as much as card or punched tape readers.

Secondly, there are devices that can sense a handwritten mark. Figure 26 shows how this can be used in an order form. The system has the severe limitation of not being able to distinguish between two different kinds of mark.

Thirdly, there are devices that can read handwritten characters directly. These are still extremely costly and, in any case, are very fussy about the quality of the writing. Opinion is divided on whether

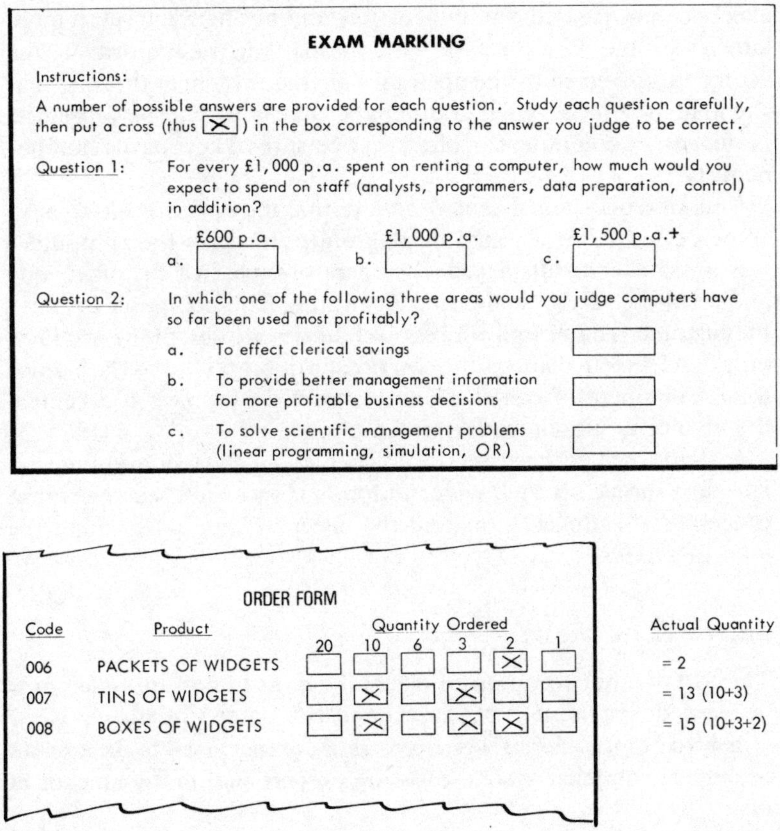

EXAM MARKING

Instructions:

A number of possible answers are provided for each question. Study each question carefully, then put a cross (thus ☒) in the box corresponding to the answer you judge to be correct.

Question 1: For every £1,000 p.a. spent on renting a computer, how much would you expect to spend on staff (analysts, programmers, data preparation, control) in addition?

a. £600 p.a. ☐ b. £1,000 p.a. ☐ c. £1,500 p.a.+ ☐

Question 2: In which one of the following three areas would you judge computers have so far been used most profitably?

a. To effect clerical savings ☐

b. To provide better management information for more profitable business decisions ☐

c. To solve scientific management problems (linear programming, simulation, OR) ☐

ORDER FORM

Code	Product	20	10	6	3	2	1	Actual Quantity
006	PACKETS OF WIDGETS	☐	☐	☐	☐	☒	☐	= 2
007	TINS OF WIDGETS	☐	☒	☐	☒	☐	☐	= 13 (10+3)
008	BOXES OF WIDGETS	☐	☒	☐	☒	☒	☐	= 15 (10+3+2)

(Quantity Ordered: 20, 10, 6, 3, 2, 1)

FIG. 26 Mark Read Documents

A 'mark reader' attached to the computer senses the presence or absence of a mark in a number of predetermined positions – indicated by the boxes.

Exam marking by this method raises an interesting discussion point. The main advantage is speed and cheapness of exam marking. It is questionable whether exams should be designed for the invigilators at the expense of limiting the self-expression of the pupils. Many commercial computer systems suffer from this type of dilemma.

there is likely to be any significant improvement in their cost and performance in the near future.

On-line input devices

Another method is key-to-disc where the output of a keyboard goes straight into the memory. The chief advantage is that many of the checks can be carried out immediately and not hours, or even days, later as is otherwise the case. This means that the majority of the errors are corrected by the operator who made them at the time that she made them – a valuable discipline that improves performance. Note that the computer can often 'service' several keyboards simultaneously.

This kind of system means, of course, that the operator has to have some device, often a visual display unit, on which the computer's messages to her are displayed. The operator types in a customer code and a set of product codes and quantities. The computer displays the customer's name and address and the description of the products on a VDU screen; displays the cost of each line; and shows the invoice total. The operator can check and correct the invoice. If accepted, the invoice is subsequently printed out.

Systems such as these are steadily becoming cheaper and the next few years should see their wider adoption. As we have seen, the input process is a feedback loop, and the faster we can cycle round the loop the better.

THE COST OF INPUT

The cost of input accounts for one of the most important differences between the economics of clerical and computer systems.

In broad terms, clerical system costs are proportional to the amount of output; computer system costs are proportional to the amount of input.

If sales statistics are produced by clerks to summarise sales figures, then each extra set of figures to be produced will cost roughly as much as the one before. If an analysis of sales by sales area costs, say, £500 in clerical labour, then an analysis of sales by television area (to assess the effectiveness of TV advertising) will cost about another £500.

If, however, the statistics are to be produced by a computer system, then the key question is: 'How much does it cost to get the raw data, that is the details of sales transactions, into the computer?' The cost of getting the details of sales coded, punched and vetted is likely to be very high. The cost of producing the report will be extremely low, consisting of a few minutes' computer time and a few yards of paper.

The corollary of this is that the more use that can be made of the computer's input, the more economic the system is likely to be – see page 20 (Chapter 2). Consider again the sales transaction – the piece of information that says that a particular customer has ordered a particular quantity of a particular item. In a fully developed system this could be used for:

advice notes and invoices
statements
reminder letters in case of non-payment
stock records
sales statistics

It is for this reason that sales accounting has often proved to be a successful computer application. For contrast, consider attendance records which are the principal input in weekly payroll applications. These records are of course necessary for calculating an employee's pay but they are entirely useless for any other purpose. Therefore the entire cost of preparing the input has to be borne by this one application and it is for this reason that weekly payroll is one of the less profitable computer applications for the average business. Its popularity despite this is due to the fact that it is an easy application in the sense that the rules for calculating a man's pay are always formalised and clearly understood and the system design process is correspondingly simple.

SUMMARY

Input is likely to be the most expensive and complex part of a computer system, in spite of various techniques to alleviate the problem. In particular, coding and error correction are ever-present headaches. Therefore, a good computer system is one in which a relatively small amount of input is used to generate a large amount of useful output.

STARTING UP

The systems have been designed, programming is complete and the time has come for the introduction of the new procedures. In some ways this is the hardest part of all. So a wise user manager will work out the timing carefully. Computer people tend to underestimate the problems of implementation and often agree to an unreasonably tight schedule. The right approach is to get a firm base by starting with a small section of the work and then to expand from there. This approach is vitally important, however difficult it may seem in practice. To 'go live' on the whole job all at once is courting disaster.

If the implementation is well planned and thought through, it will all work smoothly and without trouble. To avoid it becoming a traumatic experience, insist on five points:

1. OPERATIONS INTERFACE

During the development of new systems main contact between user and computer experts has been the systems analyst. But once the systems are in operation he will gradually drop out of the picture and the main contact will be with operations people.

You need to ensure that the flow of documents to the computer (input) and the distribution of results (output) are smooth and tested. For both input and output documents a timetable should be published showing deadlines when the work is due, how it is to be delivered and who is responsible for delivery. In addition, you will need to establish responsibilities for answering queries and resolving input difficulties.

Special problems sometimes arise when the output responsibilities are geographically separated from the input responsibilities. In these cases, a special liaison function may be needed between them. For both input and output procedures, simple manuals should be prepared containing examples of all documents with specimen entries and instructions showing what has to be done.

2. PLANNING FOR THE WORST

Plan for the worst – it usually happens, so you might as well be ready for it. Set out everything that might go wrong and then work out how it would first become noticeable and how to put it right. This applies both to the initial starting up and to routine operations. Here are some of the things that usually go wrong:

Files need amending even while they are being set up in the first place

Staff will get new procedures wrong

There will be confusion over the completing of new documents

New documents will require redesigning

Documents will get lost

Punched cards will get lost

Records will get lost on magnetic tape and disc

Documents will arrive late from branches

The new computer will have a high incidence of breakdown

The problems of handling queries will be underestimated

It will take time to bed in the new procedures – there will be problems of re-running.

3. GRADUAL IMPLEMENTATION

Do not let them put the whole payroll on to the computer one weekend – even if it is 6 April and the managing director is breathing down your neck. In all probability it will be a disaster.

Start with one small section of 50 to 100 employees and make sure all the 'bugs' are ironed out before tackling the next section. Once the system is proved, then it is possible to take on additional sections quickly. There are always good reasons why a gradual implementation is impossible. Do not listen to them.

4. PARALLEL RUNNING

Do not let your old system run down until you are satisfied the new system is working satisfactorily. It is always expensive and inconvenient to run two systems in parallel but again very necessary – the alternative is even costlier and less convenient since the risk of failure is too high.

The correct procedure is first to test the new system using historical data – say last month's transactions. When this is completely satisfactory, move on to processing current data in parallel with the old system. When this is again satisfactory, you can afford to drop the old system.

A common trap is to take on the next section before the first one is completely satisfactory. It is so easy to think that 'it is almost right, so we can move on'. **There is often a big gap between almost right and completely satisfactory.**

5. SCHEDULING

The problems of scheduling are very similar to the problems of production planning in any job shop, and since the computer is also an expensive investment it too must be used with efficiency. Schedules must be prepared which give maximum throughput while ensuring critical jobs are completed on time. The problem is more complicated on computers which allow multi-programming – running more than one job at the same time on the one computer – as this can lead to quite complicated schedules to keep job streams in balance with the power of the computer and its peripherals.

Chapter 7

Summary For Part II

Successful computer applications result from the marriage of the skills and knowledge of the computer staff and the experience of the company's managers. The partners are not likely to be completely compatible and, indeed, their relationship may have to begin with a shotgun wedding – with the chief executive's finger on the trigger.

Besides the purely technical problems in designing and programming a computer system there are the problems of:

devising the rules that the system is to apply, and where necessary, reducing discretionary powers to rules

grappling with the (often hidden) complexity of business systems

dealing with complex issues of cost/effectiveness

as far as possible, solving all these problems correctly the first time

It is clear that computer staff cannot be left to solve these problems by themselves; they must receive help and guidance from the management. Projects need careful control and monitoring to keep them on target and on time; managers must expect things to go wrong and so should plan for them; installations must not be rushed.

CHECKLIST FOR TOP MANAGEMENT

Here is a checklist of points that the chief executive should consider periodically:

1. Before a computer project goes ahead, do your staff produce firm estimates of expected costs and benefits? Do they give

serious consideration to other ways of doing the job, not involving computers? For example, when you last received a document proposing a new use for a computer, how many pages were devoted to the computer solution and how many to alternative non-computer solutions?

2. As systems design and programming work proceeds, are the estimates for costs and benefits periodically revised? If not, is it because your staff are still convinced that their original estimates were right, or is it because they are so immersed in designing the system that they have forgotten about profitability? Has any computer project in your company ever been abandoned during the design stage, as the result of the investigations made? Should any have been?

3. Are you kept informed of progress made? In particular, when the computer system becomes operational, do you get regular reports telling you what the actual costs and benefits are compared with the original estimates? And is the explanation for the discrepancy plausible?

4. What has your company's total investment been in computers? What return have you received on this investment? How does it compare with other investments you have made, or might have made?

5. Do your staff, the computer personnel themselves and the user departments feel *jointly* responsible for the success of each computer project? When an application is successful, does the user department get its fair share of the credit? In general, what is the attitude of your other managers towards the computer department and vice versa?

6. Do you expect computers to become more important or less important to your company over the next five years? If more important, is computer knowledge and experience disseminating fast enough through your company?

7. Have there been any organisational changes, such as the merging or splitting of departments, as the result of using a com-

puter? Is the responsibility for present computer applications divided up between too many people? Should you make any changes?

8. How do your computer staff spend their time? How much is spent on technical matters internal to the computer department, such as making the present programs run slightly faster, and tying up technical loose ends? How much is spent with users and potential users?

How do your computer staff spend their time?

CHECKLIST FOR MIDDLE MANAGEMENT

Here is a checklist of questions for middle management:

1. When a computer system is being designed, have you at least one member of your staff working full-time on the design team with the computer staff? Is he the right man? (If he is the right man, you will probably be experiencing considerable difficulties in continuing your day-to-day operations without him.)

2. Have you personally made any suggestions about the design of the computer system? Will they be embodied in the final system? If they were rejected, are you convinced that they should have been?

3. Have you confidence in the computer staff assigned to your project? Are you prepared to share responsibility with them for the success or failure of the project? If not, what have you done about it?

4. Are your staff properly briefed? Will they be able to work the new system? Has any training scheme been set up?

FINALLY

HOW TO ENSURE DISASTER

What follows is a list of methods for making sure that a computer installation is a failure. All have been widely used in practice; all are guaranteed.

Get a member of your staff to advise you on whether you need a computer, telling him that if the answer is 'Yes' he can be computer manager. (*Would you reasonably expect any answer other than 'yes'?*)

Buy a computer before finding a potentially profitable job for it. Buy it to gain experience in using computers, or for company prestige. (*You won't learn much that's useful, and your company's prestige will probably suffer.*)

When the computer salesman tells you that a computer will be a paying proposition, take his word for it.

Recruit staff exclusively from within your organisation whether or not they know much about computers.

Recruit staff exclusively from outside your organisation despite the fact that they know little about your business.

Leave the experts to get on with the job by themselves. You will be gratified by the brilliant results and can ignore the fact that it is very late and largely irrelevant to your real needs.

Let the experts design the systems and then get the managers to implement them. (The systems probably will not be viable, and even if they are, the managers will see to it that they fail.)

When using a computer to replace clerical staff, wait until the system is operational before deciding what staff savings are possible, thinking that you alone can withstand Parkinson's Law.

When everything goes wrong try to extricate yourself by buying a bigger and more expensive computer.

Index